JamieDeen's
GOOD FOOD

Jamie Deen's
GOOD FOOD

Cooking up a storm
with delicious,
family-friendly recipes

Jamie Deen

with Andrea Goto and Brianna Beaudry

Photography by John Kernick

Kyle Books

This book is dedicated to Moose and Bear
and the 5 o'clock girl, with all my love.

Published in 2013 by Kyle Books
www.kylebooks.com
general.enquiries@kylebooks.com

Distributed by National Book Network
4501 Forbes Blvd., Suite 200
Lanham, MD 20706
Phone: (800) 462-6420
Fax: (800) 338-4550
customercare@nbnbooks.com

10 9 8 7 6 5 4 3 2 1

ISBN 978-1-906868-97-0

Text © 2013 by Jamie Deen
Photography © 2013 by John Kernick
Book design © 2013 by Kyle Cathie Ltd

Project editor Anja Schmidt
Designer Louise Leffler
Photographer John Kernick
Food and prop styling Susie Theodorou
Copy editor Sarah Scheffel
Production Nic Jones, David Hearn, and Lisa Pinnell

Library of Congress Control No. 2013939148

Color reproduction by ALTA London
Printed and bound in China by 1010 Printing Group Ltd

CONTENTS

FOREWORD
BY PAULA DEEN

One of life's greatest joys and heartbreaks is watching your children grow up. The hurt comes with knowing that once they go out into the world you cannot protect them like you once did—you can't bandage every scrape and wipe away every tear. You simply have to trust that you've given them as much wisdom and love as possible and watch them grow. And that's where the joy comes in: seeing what happens.

Since the day he was born, Jamie has been a constant source of joy in my life. His sharp humor and kind heart draw people in. That child has never known a stranger; he'll talk the ear off anybody who'll listen, y'all. For the longest time, I wasn't sure what Jamie would make of these gifts. Let's just say he wasn't the most goal-oriented when he was in school. He more or less just rode the waves, unsure of where he'd end up. Eventually he came home to his Momma because I asked him to. I needed help starting up my first company, The Bag Lady, and I couldn't think of anyone better than my eldest son. We just about darn near killed each other in that tiny kitchen day in and day out. And when my youngest son, Bobby, joined, the three of us had to try real hard not to kill one another. One thing was clear: Jamie didn't like it. He was living my dream, not his.

Somewhere along the line, something suddenly "clicked" and Jamie found his calling closer to home than I could've ever hoped or dreamed.

We had just opened up The Lady & Sons together when Jamie fell hard for this tall, gorgeous Southern brunette who would become my daughter-in-law. He took to marriage and his budding career with a kind of maturity that I hadn't expected. He started building the life he had always wanted. Looking back, it shouldn't have surprised me that Jamie was

ready to settle down. He had always been a natural cook and charismatic leader, and he clearly craved the loving, lasting marriage that his momma and daddy didn't have. Then, when my grandbaby Jack was born, it was game over for Jamie. He threw himself headfirst into fatherhood, putting his family before anything else. Today he has two boys who both look at their father as if he hung the moon.

In between diaper changes, T-ball games, and playdates, Jamie has managed to build a successful career around food and family. He's the star of his own Food Network cooking show, *Home for Dinner*, and has now realized his dream of writing his first solo cookbook—a book that is as much about him as it is about the family who joins him at the table each and every night. Every recipe in this book has a history, many dating back generations in the Deen or Hiers families. Jamie has adapted these dishes to meet the nutritional and emotional needs of the modern family. They are full of freshness and flavor, and include locally sourced ingredients whenever possible. The recipes in this book are sure to become the ones my grandbabies will pass down to their children. And with this book, they will carry on to your family table as well.

To say that I'm proud of the cook, husband, and father Jamie has become is a real understatement, y'all. While his daddy and I tried to give our best, we didn't always have the best to give. In spite of this, Jamie has managed to live his dream, which you can see, feel, and taste in every page of this book.

And what a beautiful dream it is.

Paula Deen

INTRODUCTION

Food and family. Are there any two things that more folks, regardless of background, value?

Food was the tie that bound my family together when Bobby and I were growing up and, as adults, it has literally saved us from a lifetime of instability and countless struggles.

My mom cooked a Sunday-worthy spread just about every night of the week when Bobby and I were young boys. Unbeknownst to us, this was a by-product of her agoraphobia and an inability to leave the house. Talk about silver linings. The majority of my memories from that time are of being around the table together as a family. My mom's laughter when Bobby and I both reached for the fried chicken breasts while my poor old daddy learned to like legs and thighs. The cake Mom baked for Jesus' birthday every Christmas Eve—coconut cake, the only cake I really care to eat to this day. My daddy cutting butter into cane syrup and soaking it up with white bread for dessert. Momma, a Southern sommelier, teaching us the significance of different cornbreads and how to pair them with certain foods like they were fine wines—lacy cornbread with creamed potatoes, skillet cornbread with chili, and hoecakes with collards and pot liquor.

My memories spread out over the many different kitchens of our extended family. My Granny Paul had a tiny kitchen in her trailer on the edge of Lee County, Georgia. It wasn't even a double-wide, but the food and flavor she created there could have filled a palace. Her garden was the first dirt I ever pulled food from: potatoes, squash, tomatoes, and my favorite, fresh collard greens. Her neighbor Mr. Carr allowed Bobby and me to pick fresh strawberries from his wondrous plants of overflowing berries. I was nine years old but remember those sweet, ripe berries like we picked them yesterday. My Great Aunt Peggy's kitchen had a built-in banquet where we ate her cucumber, onion, and tomato salad. We enjoyed every meal with fresh garden veggies in oil with apple cider vinegar. I can taste it right now.

Family and food. Y'all have these memories, too.

My momma taught me that the kitchen is the heart of the home and she has never been more right. Brooke and I have two little boys who are piling up their own food memories right now. Jack, well, just turn this book over and see how food and family are shaping his life. Matthew at twenty-three months is never happier than when he is in our arms at the stove. In this family you are either gonna be a food lover or a "cooker man," as Jack used to call my occupation, but most likely you're gonna be both.

MY LIFE AS A COOKER MAN

My cooking experience is divided into five distinct stages. The first was as a prep cook—and I started young. When I was a boy I shelled peas 'til I thought my fingers were gonna fall off. Momma said, "You're gonna want to eat them, so keep shelling." With butter and fresh onions on top of white rice? Yes ma'am, I wanted to eat 'em. So I shelled and shucked and scrubbed and cleaned, building up far more memories than I did skill, which is really the point.

After this came work-for-pay. For my first job, at age fifteen, I was in charge of making cheeseburgers and also anointed head trash taker-outer. Of course, the job was at a used car auction house but, you know, a *nice* one. This period came to a close with my summer at Yellowstone National Park, where I cooked at the Old Faithful Inn. We were under the direction of the stoic chef Mike Dean—his memory still so fresh in my "kitchen mind," it's like I just saw him yesterday.

Next up was the family restaurant, The Lady & Sons. We started our business on a prayer and two hundred dollars, and have grown it into so much more than that. One bright memory is the day our self-published cookbook *Favorite Recipes from the Lady and Her Friends* was ready to be picked up from the printer. Bobby and I had slipped in a surprise dedication for Mom, and when she saw it, she just cried and cried. It was such an accomplishment for her and we were all so proud. Momma even took an unheard-of day off to recover in bed. If you ever see a copy, check us out on the back cover—we were so exhausted, we are almost unrecognizable. So many years ago, so many memories.

A few years back, I embarked on the most surprising stage: I became a "television cooker man." Bobby and I spent a summer traveling the entire country together, meeting small-business owners and featuring them and their food on our Food Network program, *Road Tasted.* Brooke was traveling with us and we were expecting Jack . . . it was such an exciting and memorable summer.

We've just wrapped shooting season two of another Food Network series, *Home for Dinner,* starring yours truly, but more important, my entire family is involved. There are too many memories associated with the show to list here, but being invited down to the field at Sanford Stadium to watch my beloved Georgia Bulldogs play football is at the top. Oh, and I've met three U.S. presidents. Thanks, TV.

But after all these years, the role I have enjoyed the most is as a "parent cooker man." From the time Brooke began making fresh baby food, we have been on a culinary carousel of wonder. There have also been stretches of hand wringing. The wants of a hungry two-year-old are known only to said toddler and they ain't saying. What I can say with certainty is that nothing beats the show a baby can put on with spaghetti. My personal mantra—turn every challenge into a positive—has been especially useful during the first years of table food. My tried-and-true advice to new parents? Introduce your kids to as many different textures and flavors as you can dream up because there are few things worse than living stuck in a chicken nugget rut.

EATING "GOOD" FOOD

So, here we are living in an age where "farm to table" is packaged like a commodity. Today there is an entire industry built around this concept, which is funny because my Granny Paul just called it "supper." The best food I've ever eaten is the food that I've watered as its roots spread into the soft Georgia soil. We keep a small garden in our yard for odds and ends we are able to cultivate. I don't even own a pair of overalls, so don't let me sound like I'm talking from my high horse, or high tractor as the case may be, but growing at least some of your own food *is* gratifying. Parents barely have time to keep our zippers up, so finding fresh food takes effort, but it's well worth it. We supplement our efforts by having a farm box of right-from-the-ground-or-vine seasonal produce delivered to our doorstep each week, and we make a habit of visiting the local farmers' market as a family on Saturday mornings.

Caring about what and how our boys eat has really changed my approach to food. We eat fresh, stock up on produce, and avoid frying foods in our home altogether. I've also started eating like a six-year-old—rather than stuffing myself whenever the feeling strikes, I keep it to three square meals a day, made up of smaller portions. As someone who grew up wearing jeans from the "husky" section, I'm happy to tell you of an unexpected bonus of cooking in this way—the most successful weight management I've ever experienced. Eat like a six-year-old, y'all, it's good for all of us.

Whether it's a big family meal at Granny Paul's trailer park or Aunt Peggy's house or an everyday dinner in my mom's kitchen or my own, food is love. Plain and simple. If I manage to inspire my kids with this message, then I'll feel I've done right by them.

CHERISHED THINGS

Two of my most cherished things live in my kitchen. One is my Granny's skillet, bought from Sears who knows how many years ago. It has hosted more chickens than a barnyard and its color has faded to an orange reminiscent of the last light of a beautiful sunset. It's my museum piece. The other is one of my sweet little momma's cutting boards. My daddy made it in his shop and it has been in my life as long as I can remember. It's the size of a bread plate and doesn't offer much more space than to cut a lemon, but I wouldn't trade it for a Cadillac.

This book you are now holding is a fantastic realization of a dream for me—my new cherished item. It's also no small miracle that, after all the obstacles our family has faced and overcome, we are still just that, a family. We love each other, we encourage each other, we push and we pull for each other, and we celebrate all the hard-fought victories, big and small. This book is a big one. Becoming a writer has always been the golden ring that I've reached for. Bobby and I first realized this dream together years ago when we published our Deen Bros. cookbook series. Sharing this accomplishment with my brother was one of the most special moments I'll ever experience, but this book here seems different. Bigger. That was our life and this is mine— my beautiful, blessed life that allows me to cover the food and people that I love most. And I'm very grateful to share this with y'all. So enough visiting, let's shake some pots.

FROM THE GROUND UP

From the Ground Up

The farm-to-table movement has gained a lot of ground recently, but let's not forget that people have been eating this way for generations. My grandmother Paul had it going on back in 1976 with her little garden of cucumbers, potatoes, tomatoes, lettuce, and the best green beans I've ever had.

In Albany, Georgia, Mom and Dad had a real big garden—about two acres—just outside of town on Aunt Peggy and Uncle George's property. I loved being outside, running between the neatly planted rows of corn, onions, and potatoes and just about every kind of lettuce you can imagine. When I got hungry, I'd pull a carrot straight from the ground, brush off the soil and eat it on the spot. Once I even dug up a perfectly intact Native American arrowhead. That garden was a pretty magical place.

The magic died down a bit when I got a little older and Bobby and I had to work the garden for a couple of summers, tilling, planting, and weeding. That's when I started to realize that it was a necessity for our families; the garden was the only reason we enjoyed fresh produce on our table every single day—leafy salads, weighted down with juicy ripe tomatoes and crisp carrots. Mom would can just about anything she could stuff into a jar—from sweet figs to pickled watermelon rinds—so our family could enjoy fruits and vegetables well into winter. The backbreaking work gave me an appreciation for fresh produce that I still have today.

My garden today doesn't come close to the size of Aunt Peggy's, but we do have fruit trees and a small container garden where Jack and I have just started to grow carrots and peppers. Jack's responsible for keeping his plants watered and weeded, and he takes his job just as seriously as Aunt Peggy did all those years. He's even learned patience from having to wait until the tomatoes are ripe enough to pick. And when he finally does get to make a big salad with the fruits and veggies he grew, he garnishes it with his favorite toppings and is so proud of what he's created—from garden to table.

That's why I've titled this chapter "From the Ground Up." Every recipe starts with something simple—chopped lettuce, chunks of watermelon, a bed of rice, or even soda crackers—and then incorporates lots of fresh vegetables and herbs. The end result is a set of flavorful, kid-pleasing recipes that reinvent the typical "garden salad," transforming it into the highlight of your family table.

FALL HARVEST SALAD WITH MAPLE VINAIGRETTE

Serves 4 to 6

Prep Time: 15 minutes
Cook Time: 30 minutes

Making the perfect salad is like walking a tightrope—it's all about balance, marrying contrasting colors, textures, and sweet and savory flavors. The roasted butternut squash gives this salad a beautiful deep-orange color and toothsome texture, while the grapes sweeten things up. The same goes for the dressing: Dijon mustard, maple syrup, and red wine vinegar—each contributes a unique kick; together they're a full-on roundhouse. By adding salty feta, which is Brooke's favorite, and pistachios, Jack's nut of choice, there's something to lure everyone to the table.

1 small butternut squash (1½ pounds), peeled, seeded, and diced

2 tablespoons olive oil

kosher salt and freshly ground black pepper

3 cups mixed baby greens

½ head radicchio, thinly sliced

1 Belgian endive, thinly sliced

1 cup seedless red grapes, sliced in half

½ cup crumbled feta

½ cup chopped salted and roasted pistachios

MAPLE VINAIGRETTE
(MAKES ABOUT ½ CUP)

½ small shallot, minced

2 tablespoons red wine vinegar

1 tablespoon real maple syrup

1 teaspoon Dijon mustard

3 tablespoons olive oil

kosher salt and freshly ground black pepper

Preheat the oven to 400°F.

Place the butternut squash on a sheet tray and drizzle with the oil. Season with salt and pepper and toss it all together. Roast for 30 minutes, giving the squash a good flip halfway through to ensure that it cooks evenly. Allow to cool to room temperature.

Meanwhile, make the maple vinaigrette: In a glass jar with a tight-fitting lid, combine the shallot, vinegar, maple syrup, Dijon, olive oil, and salt and pepper. Shake well to combine; taste and adjust seasoning.

After the squash has cooled, get yourself a large serving bowl and combine half of the butternut squash (reserve the rest for another use or nibble on it while you're preppin' the salad), the mixed greens, radicchio, endive, grapes, feta, and pistachios. Drizzle with the maple vinaigrette and toss it all together real well. Serve it up immediately.

COOKING TIPS

If your kids are adverse to sharp flavors, serve up their salad at the table before mixing in the bitter radicchio and endive.

When Jack transitioned to table food, Brooke would roast butternut squash, put it through a food processor, pour it into ice-cube trays and then freeze it so we'd always have some on hand.

Before I started cooking with butternut squash, I'd see it in the grocery and think it was a Thanksgiving decoration. Who eats a gourd? Well, I guess I do.

Broccoli is really versatile; you can eat it raw, mashed, broiled or even fried. you can cover it with melted cheese or toasted almonds. It also makes for the perfect tree in your child's kindergarten diorama.

Broccoli is one of my favorite vegetables and that's probably what turned Jack and Matthew on to it. But people tend to fall into a rut when they prepare broccoli, making it the same way they always have: steamed with butter. What we're gonna do here is make a colorful salad that's as easy to prepare as it is to pack up and carry on a picnic. The fresh crunch from the broccoli, edamame, apple, celery, and sunflower seeds pairs perfectly with the sweet, sour and smoky flavor of the bacon vinaigrette, giving this salad a flavor profile as rich as a good bottle of wine.

Bring a large pot of salted water to a boil. Add the broccoli and cook for 1 to 2 minutes, until bright green and tender-crisp. Transfer to a colander and run the broccoli under cold water until completely cool. Pat dry with a clean tea towel and transfer to a large serving bowl along with the edamame, apple, celery, sunflower seeds, and cranberries.

Meanwhile, make the bacon vinaigrette: In a medium sauté pan over medium heat, cook the bacon until the fat is rendered and the bacon is crisp, about 5 minutes. Using a slotted spoon, transfer the bacon to a paper towel–lined plate. Pour off about 1 tablespoon of the bacon fat. Add the shallot and sauté over medium heat until soft, about 1 minute. Turn off the heat and quickly whisk in the Dijon, vinegar, and brown sugar. Drizzle the salad with the dressing, add the reserved bacon, toss it really well, and season with salt and pepper.

COOKING TIP

The key is not to overcook the broccoli—that's the only way you can really mess it up. It literally only takes a minute to boil it. As soon as it turns bright green, pull it out.

CRISP BROCCOLI SALAD WITH BACON VINAIGRETTE

Serves 4 to 6

Prep time: 20 minutes
Cook time: 10 minutes

4 cups broccoli florets (from about 2 crowns)

1 cup frozen shelled edamame

1 Gala apple, or other sweet, crisp apple, peeled, cored, and chopped

2 stalks celery, sliced

$1/2$ cup roasted and salted sunflower seeds

$1/4$ cup dried cranberries

kosher salt and freshly ground black pepper

BACON VINAIGRETTE

5 slices bacon, chopped

1 medium shallot, finely chopped

1 teaspoon Dijon mustard

$1/3$ cup red wine vinegar

1 tablespoon packed light brown sugar

JACK'S FAVORITE PASTA SALAD WITH LOADS OF VEGGIES

Serves 6

Prep Time: 5 minutes
Cook Time: 15 minutes

You can use whatever pasta you like, but we often go with wagon wheels because they're Jack's favorite. I'm good with it as long as he doesn't think it's hilarious to roll 'em across the table during dinnertime.

This dish gets more play at our house than any other recipe in the book because it's easy and everybody loves it. We'll have it once a week as a main course without fail. It's so satisfying—it's like I'm taking the entire food pyramid and tossing it into a bowl. This recipe's got vegetables, grains, dairy, a bit of oil, fruit (tomato counts), and you can easily add a protein such as chopped-up grilled chicken if you want. You can also exchange any of the vegetables for ones that you and your kids prefer. Sometimes I'll dress up my bowl with pine nuts or olives, while keeping my kids' dish pretty traditional. This attention to their preferences makes for a more peaceful dining experience for everyone!

12 ounces wagon wheel pasta

1 cup frozen shelled edamame

2 carrots, well scrubbed and cut into ½-inch chunks

1 broccoli crown (12 ounces), cut into bite-size florets

1 cup grape tomatoes, sliced in half

1 cup shredded part-skim mozzarella

3 tablespoons olive oil

2 tablespoons red wine vinegar

¼ cup mayonnaise

1 teaspoon sugar

kosher salt and freshly ground black pepper

Add the pasta to a large pot of boiling salted water. Cook the pasta for 3 minutes less than recommended on the back of package. When the timer goes off, add the edamame and carrots and cook for 2 minutes longer. Next, add the broccoli and continue boiling for 1 minute more.

Drain the pasta and veggies in a colander. Rinse really well under cold water to stop the cooking process. (Make sure you drain off all the liquid so you don't water down your salad.) Transfer the pasta and veggies to a large serving bowl, along with the tomatoes and mozzarella.

Combine the oil, vinegar, mayonnaise, sugar, and salt and pepper in a jam jar and shake it until it's all mixed up. Taste and adjust seasoning.

Pour the dressing over the pasta, toss well, and serve warm, though you can make ahead if you need to.

GRILLED RAINBOW CHOPPED SALAD

Serves 6

Prep time: 10 minutes
Cook time: 10 minutes

Remember the days when the only people who ate salads were skinny girls who complained they were fat? Back then salads were a punishment. At best, they were used as a stall tactic as you waited for the meal you actually wanted. But over the years, we've all come to realize that there's so much more to salad than a head of iceberg lettuce. In fact, this recipe is the best example of what a salad should aspire to be: full of color, flavor, and texture. And because I still get to work the grill, no one questions my manhood when I want a salad for dinner.

1 medium zucchini, sliced in half lengthwise

1 medium orange bell pepper, sliced into quarters

1 small red onion, sliced into $1/2$-inch-thick rings

2 ears of corn, husked

2 tablespoons olive oil

kosher salt and freshly ground black pepper

1 cup grape tomatoes, sliced in half

1 large ripe avocado, pitted and diced

$1/4$ cup loosely packed fresh basil leaves, torn

1 romaine heart, chopped

2 cups loosely packed baby arugula

LEMONY DIJON DRESSING

2 teaspoons Dijon mustard

juice of $1/2$ lemon

3 tablespoons extra-virgin olive oil

kosher salt and freshly ground black pepper

Heat your outdoor grill or grill pan to medium-high.

Place the zucchini, bell pepper, onion, and corn on a sheet tray, drizzle with the oil, and season with salt and pepper. Add the veggies to the grill and cook them for 8 to 10 minutes, rotating so all sides are evenly cooked. Remove the vegetables from the grill and let them sit just until they're cool to the touch. Chop the zucchini, bell pepper, and onion into bite-size pieces and cut the corn kernels off the cobs. Transfer the grilled chopped vegetables to a large serving bowl. Add the tomatoes, avocado, basil, romaine, and arugula.

To make the dressing, combine the Dijon, lemon juice, olive oil, and salt and pepper in a jam jar and shake well to combine; taste and adjust the seasoning. Pour your dressing over the salad and toss it together. Serve immediately.

This "salad" is probably the craziest-sounding recipe that you'll find in this book, but you've got to try it. Trust me, it's like egg salad on steroids. We used to make this for our sack lunches back when we had The Bag Lady because it was so easy to throw together. You're literally making something out of nothing. The few ingredients it calls for are things most people already have on hand: soda crackers (I use good ol' Saltines), tomatoes, celery, onions, mayonnaise, and eggs. The result is a creamy side salad that pairs especially well with soup or a sandwich at lunchtime and Oven-Fried Flounder Filets (page 116) at dinner. Your friends and family will never guess what they're eating, and I promise they'll never forget this dish, either—for all the right reasons.

OLD FASHIONED SODA CRACKER SALAD

Serves 6

Prep Time: 10 minutes
Cook Time: zero

In a medium bowl, crush up the crackers by hand to get a nice chunky texture. Add the rest of the ingredients, mix well, and serve immediately.

1 sleeve soda crackers (4 ounces)

1 plum tomato, finely chopped

2 stalks celery (including leaves), diced

4 green onions, finely chopped

1 cup mayonnaise

4 hard-boiled eggs, finely chopped

The only way you can screw this up is by letting it sit too long. Its lifespan is 10 to 15 minutes. I mean, it's mayonnaise on crackers, y'all.

WATERMELON, FETA, AND MINT SALAD

Serves 6

Prep time: 15 minutes
Cook time: Zero

½ small red onion, thinly sliced

2 tablespoons rice wine vinegar

2 tablespoons sunflower or canola oil

kosher salt and freshly ground black pepper

½ seedless watermelon (4 pounds), sliced or cubed

⅓ cup crumbled feta cheese

⅓ cup fresh mint leaves, torn

My cousin introduced me to dipping carrots in yellow mustard, which sounds real weird, but tastes surprisingly good. This salad definitely falls into the "mustard-on-a-carrot" category.

Watermelon, onion, feta and mint may seem like a strange flavor combination, but then you taste it and wonder why you ever questioned it. Besides being super pretty—the white feta and green mint pop against the pink of the watermelon flesh—it's a perfectly light and refreshing dish that you can take to a baby shower or picnic. And you don't have to bother with leftovers; Brooke always comes home with an empty bowl.

Place the onion in a large serving bowl and drizzle with the vinegar and oil; season with a big pinch of salt and pepper. Toss everything together and let the onion marinate for 5 minutes so it softens and loses some of its bite. Then add the watermelon, feta, and mint and toss really well. Serve immediately.

COOKING TIP

You don't want to make this salad too far ahead of time. I suggest serving it immediately after you dress it or the watermelon will start to get slimy. If transporting, bring your tossed onions and watermelon, mint and feta separately and toss together on site.

SOUP
KITCHEN

Soup Kitchen

Soups and stews have always been a big part of my family's cooking. When I was a kid, Mom made them because they were easy, affordable, and always yielded a ton. We'd happily eat soup for a couple of days because it would get better and better the longer it stayed in the fridge. Her chicken and rice soup rarely lasted more than two days because we loved it so much, but if it did, Mom would freeze the leftovers in small containers for quick, go-to lunches.

I've always been a chili and beef stew kind of guy—the heartier the soup, the better—and if I were still a single guy, these would be all that I'd cook. But thank goodness Brooke came along and introduced me to things like grooming products, dryer sheets, and the goodness of lighter soups. You can really see her influence in this chapter. While I still include recipes like Creamy Roasted Broccoli Soup and my World's Best Chili (which is guaranteed to win in any cook-off), Brooke encouraged me to develop a number of lighter recipes with just as much flavor, including Kale and White Bean Soup and, her personal favorite, Brooke's Easy Egg-Drop Soup.

Like my mom, I take great joy in cooking my family a big, comforting pot of soup that takes four hours to slow-cook on the stove, but I just don't have that kind of time during the week. So, all of the recipes in this chapter take very little time to prepare and yet they taste delicious. If you still crave a simmer-all-day soup, just follow Mom's advice and make extra to store in the freezer where the flavors can sit and marry together for up to six months. Now that's love.

GINGERY BUTTERNUT SQUASH BISQUE

Serves 6

Prep time: 15 minutes
Cook time: 35 minutes

2 tablespoons olive oil

1 medium onion, chopped

2 cloves garlic, chopped

1 (2-inch) piece fresh ginger, peeled and
chopped (about 2¹/₂ tablespoons)

¹/₄ teaspoon ground cinnamon

dash of freshly grated nutmeg

kosher salt and freshly ground black pepper

1 quart Homemade Chicken Stock (page 205)

1 cup apple juice

1 cup water

1 large butternut squash (3 pounds), peeled,
seeded, and cut into 1-inch chunks

1 Granny Smith apple, peeled, cored,
and chopped

sour cream for serving (optional)

An added bonus: If this soup does end up on the ceiling, it will clean up rather nicely.

Proof that butternut squash has a flavor with universal appeal: It was the first solid food both my boys ate—and liked. I know, because it didn't end up on the ceiling. So, we've served butternut a lot of different ways in our house. This soup is one of my favorites because it packs so many sweet and savory flavors into every spoonful. The fresh chopped ginger gives this creamy soup a touch of heat that's balanced by the sweetness of the apple. It makes for a satisfying weeknight meal, although it could just as easily hold its own at a dinner party. (After having kids we never actually host dinner parties, but I just know it would be great.)

Heat the oil in a large saucepan over medium-high heat. Once it's hot, add the onion and cook, stirring, until tender, about 3 minutes. Stir in the garlic and ginger, and continue cooking for 2 minutes more, until real fragrant. Sprinkle in the cinnamon, nutmeg, and salt and pepper, and continue cooking and stirring for about 1 minute more. Pour in the stock, juice, and water, and bring the liquid up to a good simmer. Add the squash and apple, bring to a boil, reduce the heat to a simmer, and cook on medium heat for about 30 minutes, or until the squash is tender.

Transfer the soup to a blender, in batches, and puree until smooth. Return the soup back to the pot you started with and bring it back up to a low simmer. Serve in warm bowls, with a small dollop of sour cream swirled in for added creaminess, if y'all like.

COOKING TIP

Kid-appeal aside, this is an elegant soup that would do just fine at the Thanksgiving table. It looks very pretty with some sour cream swirled into the bowl, or go the extra inch and top the soup with crumbled goat cheese.

ROASTED TOMATO SOUP WITH GRILLED CHEESE CROUTONS

Serves 6 to 8

Prep time: 5 minutes
Cooking time: 1 hour 5 minutes

Drowning grilled cheese croutons in soup is my grown-up way of eatin' like a kid.

Making tomato soup that comes right out of a can is fine, and believe me, there have been a few hurry-up-and-eat nights when I've done just that. But it can't compete with this roasted tomato version made from scratch. I add a squeeze of my favorite local honey and a sweet Vidalia onion that's grown just about an hour from us here in Savannah. These fresh ingredients give the soup layers of flavor that you just can't find in a can. The grilled cheese croutons came about as a kind of compromise. I'm a "dunker"—I use a sandwich instead of a soup spoon—but Brooke can't stand soggy bread. So I serve her croutons on the side and sprinkle mine on top.

3 pounds plum tomatoes, cut in half

1 Vidalia onion, cut into quarters

6 cloves garlic, smashed but not peeled

3 tablespoons olive oil

1 tablespoon honey

kosher salt and freshly ground black pepper

1 quart Homemade Chicken Stock (page 205)

1 tablespoon chopped fresh dill,
plus more for serving

Grilled Cheese Croutons (recipe follows)

COOKING TIP

Roasting the tomatoes brings out their natural sweetness and adds depth of flavor. The honey kicks up the sweetness a notch.

Preheat the oven to 425°F.

Place the tomatoes, onion, and garlic on a heavy-bottomed sheet tray. Drizzle with the oil and honey and season with a good-size pinch of salt and pepper. Toss everything together with your hands and roast in the oven for 35 to 40 minutes, or until the tomatoes are soft and beginning to caramelize on the edges.

Slip the garlic cloves out of their skins. Using a slotted spoon, scoop the vegetables, in batches, into a blender. Puree until smooth.

Place the sheet tray on a burner and add about $^3/_4$ cup stock to the pan. Scrape up any browned bits with a wooden spoon and bring the liquid to a simmer. Transfer to a large saucepan along with the remaining $3^1/_4$ cups stock and puree. Season well with salt and pepper and simmer for 25 minutes. During the last few minutes of cooking, stir in the dill. Serve with Grilled Cheese Croutons and another sprinkle of chopped dill.

GRILLED CHEESE CROUTONS

Serves 4

Prep time: 5 minutes
Cooking time: 6 minutes

4 slices sourdough bread, sliced about $^1/_2$ inch thick

1 cup grated sharp yellow cheddar cheese

2 tablespoons butter, softened

Heat a large nonstick skillet over medium-high heat.

Evenly sprinkle two slices of bread with the cheese and sandwich each with a second slice of bread. Butter the outsides of each sandwich and cook until golden and crisp on both sides, about 3 minutes per side. Remove from the pan and let rest for 1 minute before cutting with a serrated knife into 2-inch-square croutons.

BROOKE'S EASY EGG-DROP SOUP

Serves 3 to 4

Prep time: 5 minutes
Cook time: 15 minutes

This soup is something Brooke always orders when we go out for Chinese and I was surprised how easy it is to make at home. Like any hot soup, it's literally a great warm-up to a meal, especially if it's accompanying a dish from the same family, geographically speaking, like a stir-fry or Asian tuna burger (see page 56). Or bulk up this soup by adding a few handfuls of baby spinach, chopped leftover chicken, and shelled peas or edamame to the broth, turning a first course into a main one.

1 quart Homemade Chicken Stock (page 205)
1 (1-inch) piece fresh ginger, thinly sliced
1 teaspoon reduced-sodium soy sauce
$1/8$ teaspoon ground white pepper
1 tablespoon cornstarch
2 large eggs, lightly beaten
2 green onions, thinly sliced

In a medium saucepan over medium-high heat, combine the stock, ginger, soy sauce, and pepper. Bring to a boil, then reduce the heat to medium and simmer for 10 minutes. Remove the ginger with a slotted spoon and discard.

In a small bowl, whisk the cornstarch in about $1/4$ cup of the hot broth to create a slurry. Pour the slurry into the pan of simmering stock, all the while whisking. In about a minute, the broth should thicken up. Turn off the heat and swirl the broth with a wooden spoon to create a whirlpool effect and slowly pour in the eggs. The eggs will cook in about a minute. Stir in the green onions just before you're ready to sit down to eat.

INGREDIENT NOTE

Don't be turned off by the cornstarch in the soup. It thickens up the soup to add a bit of viscosity.

DAD'S CAULIFLOWER, BEER, AND CHEDDAR SOUP

Serves 4 to 6

Prep time: 10 minutes
Cook time: 25 minutes

Savannah hosts the second largest St. Patrick's Day celebration next to New York City, so there are plenty of potlucks to prep for. When made with Guinness and Irish cheddar, this soup is like a pot o' gold.

Back in the day, when Brooke and I could try new restaurants without considering how they ranked on the kid-friendly meter, we went to a place that served a cheddar and beer dip that we both fell hard for. Y'all, if we could've put a straw in that dip without anyone noticing, I think we would've. I got to thinking about how I could turn that dip into something we could slurp down without getting strange looks. So I took one of my favorite soups—cauliflower—and introduced beer and cheddar flavors to create a thick, rich soup we both would enjoy. The straw's optional.

4 tablespoons butter

1 medium onion, chopped

1 stalk celery, chopped

1 carrot, peeled and chopped

kosher salt and freshly ground black pepper

3 tablespoons all-purpose flour

4 cups low-sodium or Homemade Chicken Stock (page 205)

1 cup dark beer

1 medium head cauliflower (1½ pounds), cored and chopped

1 tablespoon Dijon mustard

1 teaspoon hot sauce

1 cup grated extra-sharp white cheddar cheese (4 ounces)

Melt the butter in a large, heavy-bottomed saucepan. Once it's foamy, add the onion, celery, and carrot and sauté until tender, about 3 minutes. Season with some salt and pepper and sprinkle the flour over the vegetables. Cook, while stirring, for 2 minutes.

Whisk in the stock and beer, bring to a boil, reduce the heat to a simmer, and then add the cauliflower. Simmer for 15 minutes, until the cauliflower is super tender.

Remove from the heat and stir in the Dijon and hot sauce. Transfer the soup to a blender in batches and puree until velvety smooth. Return the soup to the pot and bring it back up to a low simmer. The final step is to stir in the cheddar cheese by the handful, making sure each addition is melted and smooth before putting in more.

COOKING TIP

If you're looking for a lower-calorie soup, this recipe is surprisingly delicious even without the cheese.

Sadly, the parsnip has been treated like a second-class carrot for too long. I've been putting it in dishes that traditionally call for carrots and the result is a spicy, amped-up flavor in an otherwise classic recipe.

A big pot of stew always makes for a perfect family meal because it's savory, satisfying, and easy to throw together. I consider this dish a foundation recipe because you can use it to create a number of different meals, experimenting with the ingredients you have on hand. For example, this velvety full-bodied stew is really good over rice or as a filling for a puff pastry. Or you can put it in a baking dish and top with puff pastry, transforming this recipe into a delicious potpie.

HEARTY BEEF STEW WITH ROASTED PARSNIPS AND POTATOES

Serves 6

Prep time: 20 minutes
Cook time: 3 hours 5 minutes

In a large Dutch oven over medium heat, cook the bacon, stirring, until nice and crisp, about 4 minutes. Using a slotted spoon, transfer to a paper towel–lined plate. Pat the beef dry with a paper towel and season with salt and pepper on all sides. Add 2 tablespoons of the oil and the beef to the pot, in batches, and brown well on all sides. Transfer to a large plate.

Add the onion and garlic to the pot and cook until the onion is just beginning to turn golden brown, about 5 minutes. Sprinkle in some salt and pepper, then stir in the tomato paste. Cook for 2 minutes, then stir in the stock and vinegar. Add the bay leaf and thyme and return the beef to the pot. Bring the stew up to a boil, then reduce to a simmer, cover with a lid, and cook for a good $2^{1}/_{2}$ hours, until the beef is fork-tender, stirring on occasion.

About an hour before the beef has finished cooking, preheat the oven to 400°F. Place the parsnips and potatoes on a sheet tray and drizzle them with the remaining 2 tablespoons oil. Season with salt and pepper and roast for 35 to 40 minutes, until browned and tender, flipping with a spatula halfway through cooking. Just 5 minutes before serving time, remove the bay leaf and stir the roasted parsnips and potatoes into the stew.

INGREDIENT NOTES

Beef chuck is great for stews. It's a tough cut of meat with lots of connective tissue that melts when cooked low and slow. Look for red meat that's marbled with fat. While I like the subtle spicy flavor the parsnips provide, feel free to roast your family's favorite root vegetables.

4 slices bacon, cut into $^{1}/_{2}$-inch pieces

2 pounds beef chuck, trimmed of visible fat and cut into $1^{1}/_{2}$-inch cubes

kosher salt and freshly ground black pepper

$^{1}/_{4}$ cup olive oil

1 large Vidalia onion, chopped

4 cloves garlic, peeled and smashed

1 can (6 ounces) tomato paste

1 quart low-sodium or Homemade Chicken Stock (page 205)

1 tablespoon balsamic vinegar

1 bay leaf

4 sprigs fresh thyme

3 parsnips, cut into 1-inch chunks, halved if thick

1 pound medium Yukon gold potatoes, well scrubbed and quartered

KALE AND WHITE BEAN SOUP

Serves 6

Prep Time: 10 minutes
Cook Time: 40 minutes

This chunky soup is a perfectly satisfying supper for a cold night. Hearty enough to be dinner on its own when served with a green salad and some good crusty bread.

This soup borrows from that Southern tradition, making a warm, hearty meal that's perfect for fall—or, as I prefer to call it, football season. But unlike heavy chowders and meaty chilis, this broth-based soup is really good for you. If you haven't had much experience with kale, now is the time to get to know her. Dubbed the "queen of greens," this close relative of collard greens could take spinach in an arm-wrestling match any day. It's one of the healthiest vegetables on the planet; one cup of kale gets you 180% of the daily requirement of vitamin A, 200% of vitamin C, and a whopping 1,020% of vitamin K. Just knowing that makes me feel like I could leap over a building with a single bound.

1 tablespoon olive oil

12 ounces sweet Italian turkey sausage, casings removed

1 medium onion, finely chopped

2 cloves garlic, finely chopped

1 1/2 cups Homemade Chicken Stock (page 205)

1 can (14 1/2 ounces) diced tomatoes

1 can (15 1/2 ounces) white beans, drained and rinsed

kosher salt and freshly ground black pepper

1 bunch kale, tough stems removed, leaves chopped into 1/2-inch pieces

freshly grated Parmesan cheese for serving

crusty bread for serving (optional)

Heat the oil in a large soup pot over medium-high heat. Once it's hot, add the sausage and cook until browned, stirring and breaking up the meat as best you can with the back of your spoon, 3 to 4 minutes.

Add the onion and sauté until tender, just about 3 minutes. Stir in the garlic and sauté until the aromas really start to come out, just 1 to 2 minutes more. Pour in the stock, tomatoes with their juices, and beans, and season it all with a big pinch of salt and pepper. Bring the soup to a simmer, then stir in the kale by big handfuls. Simmer over medium heat for 30 minutes, stirring on occasion.

Serve each bowl topped with some Parmesan along with some crusty bread to sop up the goods.

INGREDIENT NOTE

Kale can be a bitter woman. If you prefer a milder flavor, opt for smaller leaves. Either way, look for firm, deeply colored leaves with hardy stems.

WORLD'S BEST CHILI

Serves 6 to 8

Prep time: 15 minutes
Cook time: 2 hours 15 minutes

2 tablespoons olive oil

1 large red onion, diced

2 medium bell peppers (green and red), diced

2 stalks celery, diced

5 cloves garlic, chopped

1 1/2 pounds lean ground beef

1/4 cup chili powder

1 tablespoon ground cumin

1 tablespoon dried oregano

1/2 teaspoon cayenne pepper

1 can (6 ounces) tomato paste

1 can (28 ounces) diced tomatoes

1 can (14 1/2 ounces) fire-roasted diced tomatoes

1 can (12 ounces) beer

2 cans (15 ounces each) kidney beans, drained and rinsed

1 can (15 ounces) pinto beans, drained and rinsed

shredded cheddar cheese for serving (optional)

sour cream for serving (optional)

chopped green onions for serving (optional)

I've been a judge at more than my share of chili cook-offs, so I know that everybody's got their secret this or that to make a prize-winning stew. But honestly, y'all, I've yet to taste one that beats the recipe I came up with about fifteen years ago. I was asked to do a cooking demonstration for a wonderful organization called The Living Vine, which assists expectant mothers who are facing some real challenges in their lives. I decided to teach the women how to make chili; since most of the ingredients come from a can, it's simple and inexpensive, but also incredibly satisfying. The recipe was so popular that they published it on their website and named it "The Living Vine Chili." To this day, I still get calls from people who've won competitions with that recipe.

Heat the oil in a large Dutch oven over medium-high heat. Once the oil is hot, add the onion, peppers, and celery and sauté until soft, about 4 minutes. Add the garlic and sauté for 1 to 2 minutes, just until fragrant. Stir in the beef, breaking it up with the back of your wooden spoon, and cook until browned, about 5 minutes. Stir in the chili powder, cumin, oregano, and cayenne and sauté for about 2 minutes more. Stir the tomato paste into the beef; this will intensify the flavor. Add both cans of diced tomatoes with their juices, the beer, and all the beans, stirring to combine. Bring the chili to a boil, then reduce to a simmer, cover with a lid, and cook on medium-low for a good 2 hours, stirring on occasion to keep the chili from sticking to the bottom of the pan.

If you like, top each bowl with cheddar, sour cream, and green onions before serving.

COOKING TIP

One of the best things about making a big pot of chili is that you can freeze the leftovers. All the flavors will continue to marry together so it'll be even better when you reheat it.

This version here includes one of my favorite ingredients, beer.

SUPER-SIMPLE LEMON CHICKEN AND RICE SOUP

Serves 8

Prep time: 10 minutes
Cook time: 30 minutes

I'm surprised to see how many people turn to a can for comfort food. When the sniffles hit you, the last thing you want is a runny, colorless concoction of condensed anything. Instead, take just a few extra minutes (literally) to cook up a warm bowl of this homemade chicken and rice soup. The lemon juice gives it a bright, zesty flavor. It'll cure you, guaranteed.

2 tablespoons olive oil

1 medium onion, finely chopped

2 large carrots, peeled and cut into half moons

kosher salt and freshly ground black pepper

1 quart Homemade Chicken Stock (page 205)

2 cups water

juice of 2 lemons (about $^1/_2$ cup)

$^1/_2$ cup long-grain rice

1 bay leaf

2 cups chopped leftover cooked chicken

2 tablespoons chopped fresh parsley

Heat the oil in a large soup pot over medium-high heat. Once it's hot, add the onion and carrots and sauté until tender, about 4 minutes. Season with salt and pepper and pour in the stock, water, and lemon juice. Bring it all to a boil, then stir in the rice, add the bay leaf, and knock down the heat to a simmer. Cook for 20 minutes, until the rice and carrots are tender. Stir in the chicken and cook for just a few minutes longer, until the chicken is heated through. Sprinkle in the parsley and give a taste for seasoning, adding salt and pepper if it needs it. Remove the bay leaf before serving.

CREAMY ROASTED BROCCOLI SOUP

Serves 4 to 6

Prep time: 15 minutes
Cook time: 35 minutes

With just a little bit of olive oil and a dash of salt and pepper, roasted vegetables have a sweet, full-bodied taste that will trump boiled veggies any day. So here I've taken that fantastic flavor and turned it into a smooth and creamy broccoli soup—it's one of Brooke's favorites. What you lose in color during roasting, you'll more than make up in flavor.

2 small bunches broccoli crowns (about 1$^3/_4$ pounds)

1 medium onion, chopped

3 tablespoons olive oil

kosher salt and freshly ground black pepper

1$^1/_2$ cups Homemade Chicken Stock (page 205)

2 tablespoons freshly grated Parmesan cheese

$^1/_2$ cup heavy cream

shredded cheddar cheese for serving (optional)

Preheat the oven to 425°F.

Trim the broccoli and chop the stems into $^1/_2$-inch pieces; cut the top into bite-sized florets. Place the broccoli and onion on a rimmed sheet tray and drizzle with the oil. Season with salt and pepper and toss it all together. Roast until the broccoli is cooked through and golden brown in spots, 20 to 25 minutes, tossing halfway through.

A few minutes before the broccoli is finished roasting, bring the stock up to a simmer in a medium soup pot. Add the broccoli to the simmering broth and cook for 10 minutes, to allow the flavors to marry together.

Transfer the soup to a blender in batches and puree until it's real smooth. Return the soup to the pot and bring to a low simmer. Stir in the Parmesan cheese and heavy cream. Serve in bowls and sprinkle with some cheddar, if you like.

HAND HOLDIN'

Hand Holdin'

I've been in the food industry for more than twenty-five years, and as a result, I can sear a steak and supreme an orange with the best of 'em. But I'm still that guy who finds certain domestic tasks a little tedious—such as making my bed and washing dishes. I'm only going to be out of that bed for a few hours and I'm going to use a plate and fork at least three times a day, so I feel like I'm constantly tidying up, just to mess things up again. It's not that I'm lazy—quite the opposite. I'm a married man with a restaurant to run, a TV show to shoot, and a million commitments in between. Add in two kids and a bulldog with respiratory challenges and life starts to get real crazy, real fast.

Enter the sandwich. The sandwich is God's gift to anyone who's constantly on the run. The cleanup is minimal—the portability, maximized. I'm actually able to eat with one hand and make work calls, play with action figures, and clean up dog drool with the other.

I was first introduced to the art of the sandwich back in college, when I spent a summer working at Yellowstone National Park. A buddy and I worked in the pantry kitchen at the Old Faithful Inn, where all we did was make soups and sandwiches for the two million people who went through the park. I'd have a ham sandwich for breakfast just as often as I'd have one for lunch, just because it was so quick and simple.

Surprisingly, I never tired of sandwiches and it's a good thing, because by the time I returned from Yellowstone, Momma was set to launch The Bag Lady, where we bagged around 250 sandwiches a day. We started off with the basics—ham, turkey, and egg salad sandwiches. It was good, simple food that was no trouble to make. But as the business started to boom, Mom got inspired, putting things like grilled chicken and Boston pork butt on homemade buns—and the rest is history.

The recipes in this chapter are a reflection of my long-standing affair with the sandwich. They run the gamut, from the Four Pillars (see page 63), which were the foundation for The Bag Lady, to more contemporary and complex fare like Asian-Style Tuna Burgers and Southwestern Turkey Clubs with Chipotle Mayo. Every recipe comes with a homemade topping that takes something ordinary—like mayo and coleslaw—and transforms it into something extraordinary when it's loaded onto these fork-free dishes.

Plates optional. Napkins required.

HOMEMADE BLACK BEAN BURGERS WITH FRESH PICO DE GALLO

Makes 4 burgers

Prep time: 20 minutes
Cook time: 20 minutes

A very satisfying veggie burger. I like having them for leftovers for lunch, too. Just a quick reheat in the microwave and your lunch is ready to go.

If you would've told me twenty years ago that I'd eat—and enjoy—a black bean burger, I would've slapped you upside the head with a quarter pounder. Black bean burgers were for sorority girls, not a meat eater like myself. I was reintroduced to black beans while working in our restaurant, where we served them with crab cakes. I spent many a day hunched over the stove, tweaking the seasoning so that the beans had just enough bite without overpowering the crab cakes. These black bean patties are a twist on my mom's old recipe. Growing up, she'd make us what she called bean-cake sandwiches. Come to think of it, Momma made cakes out of just about anything—corn, black-eyed peas, butter (y'all gotta try her Gooey Butter Cake)—so I guess it's only natural for me to make a savory bean sandwich for my boys as well. I've added edamame to the mix for a pop of green and topped it all off with homemade Fresh Pico de Gallo, which is sure to earn Jack and Matthew some future points from the sorority girls . . .

¼ cup olive oil

½ small red onion, finely chopped

1 large carrot, diced

3 cloves garlic, minced

1 tablespoon chili powder

½ teaspoon smoked paprika

kosher salt and freshly ground black pepper

2 cans (14½ ounces each) black beans, drained and rinsed

¾ cup frozen shelled edamame, thawed

1 large egg, beaten

4 soft whole-wheat hamburger buns, toasted

sour cream for topping

Fresh Pico de Gallo (recipe opposite)

Heat 2 tablespoons of the oil in a large nonstick skillet over medium heat. Once the oil is hot, add the onion and carrot and cook until softened, about 4 minutes. Stir in the garlic, chili powder, and paprika, and continue cooking for 1 minute more. Season the mixture with a big pinch of salt and pepper. Toss in the black beans and edamame and give it all a good stir. Remove the bean mixture from the heat and scrape it into a bowl; let it all cool to room temperature.

Once it's cool, transfer the bean mixture to a food processor. Give it a good pulse, but make sure it stays chunky (y'all don't want it to be smooth). Stir in the egg and season lightly with salt and pepper. Press the mixture into four 4-inch patties.

Wipe your skillet clean with some paper towels, then heat the remaining 2 tablespoons oil in it over medium heat. Once it's hot, add the patties, reduce the heat to medium, and cook for about 5 minutes on each side, just until they're browned and crisp. Sandwich the burgers on the toasted buns and top with the sour cream and Pico de Gallo.

FRESH PICO DE GALLO

Combine all of the ingredients together in a mixing bowl and season with 2 big pinches of salt. Let the Pico de Gallo sit out at room temperature for about 20 minutes to really get the flavors to marry before serving.

To me, cilantro tastes like soap. But if y'all are fans of that squeaky-clean flavor, feel free to add some.

Makes 2 1/2 cups

Prep time: 20 minutes
Cook time: zero

6 plum tomatoes, diced (about 1 1/2 pounds)

1 clove garlic, minced

1 small jalapeño, seeded and finely diced

1/2 small red onion, finely diced

1 1/2 teaspoons olive oil

zest and juice of 1 lime

kosher salt

SOUTHWESTERN TURKEY CLUBS WITH CHIPOTLE MAYO

Makes 2 sandwiches

Prep time: 15 minutes
Cook time: 15 minutes

Here, I've downsized the original club so you can actually get your mouth around it, but if you want to double stack, that's your call.

The traditional turkey club sandwich seems to be a featured item on just about every golf-club menu across the country. I had this Southwestern version when I was in California—and true to form, that sandwich was stacked as high as my handicap and held together by four toothpicks working overtime. It's the perfect sandwich because it includes so many textures and flavors—it's got the pickled jalapeños, the creamy pepper Jack cheese, and homemade Chipotle Mayo, which gives plain ol' mayonnaise a kick in the pants. (The guacamole and butter lettuce keep the heat in check.)

8 slices bacon

10 slices smoked turkey (from the deli counter)

4 slices nice white bread, toasted

4 deli slices pepper Jack cheese

1 plum tomato, sliced

2 tablespoons pickled jalapeños, sliced

4 leaves butter lettuce

Chunky Guacamole (recipe page 62)

CHIPOTLE MAYO

1 tablespoon canned chipotle chiles, chopped

1/2 cup mayonnaise

kosher salt and freshly ground black pepper

Preheat the oven to 400°F.

Arrange the bacon on a foil-lined sheet tray and bake for 18 to 20 minutes, or until crisp. Drain the bacon on a paper towel–lined plate.

Meanwhile, make the chipotle mayo: Mash the chiles, mayonnaise, and salt and pepper to taste in a small bowl until smooth.

Divide the turkey between two slices of bread, layering each with two slices of bacon and two slices of pepper Jack. Top with the tomato slices, pickled jalapeños, and butter lettuce. Spread the remaining two slices of bread with the chipotle mayo, then the guacamole. Close up each sandwich and slice in half for serving.

BLACKENED FRESH CATCH SANDWICHES WITH EASY TARTAR SAUCE AND PICKLED RED ONIONS

Makes 4 sandwiches

Prep time: 5 minutes
Cook time: 10 minutes

Taking the time to pickle red onions and make my own tartar sauce gives this sandwich a fresh homemade flavor that you're just not going to find when throwing a piece of fish on a hoagie roll. To taste the difference, take the time to do something different—and by "time" I mean fifteen minutes, tops. Tilapia, red snapper, or grouper would all work here.

1 tablespoon kosher salt

2 teaspoons freshly ground black pepper

1 teaspoon cayenne pepper

2 teaspoons smoked paprika

2 teaspoons garlic powder

4 catfish filets (6 ounces each)

2 tablespoons canola oil

Tartar Sauce (see right)

4 (8-inch) sesame hoagie rolls, toasted

Pickled Red Onions (see right)

1 small avocado, pitted and thinly sliced

1 cup shredded iceberg lettuce or baby arugula

In a small bowl, whisk together the salt, pepper, cayenne, smoked paprika, and garlic powder. Generously sprinkle both sides of the fish with the spice mixture.

Heat a large cast-iron skillet over medium-high heat. Add the oil and, once it's hot, add the fish, cooking on each side until blackened and cooked through, about 4 minutes on each side.

Spread tartar sauce on both sides of the rolls. Place the blackened fish filet on the bottom of each roll and top with the pickled red onions, avocado slices, and shredded lettuce or arugula. Close the hoagie rolls and serve.

TARTAR SAUCE
Makes about 1 cup

Prep time: 5 minutes   Cook time: zero

1 cup mayonnaise

1/4 cup dill pickle relish

1 tablespoon lemon juice

dash of hot sauce

kosher salt and freshly ground black pepper

Mix together all the ingredients in a small bowl. Season with salt and pepper to taste. The sauce can be stored in the refrigerator in a covered container for up to 1 week.

PICKLED RED ONIONS
Makes 2 cups

Prep time: 5 minutes   Cook time: 5 minutes

1 1/2 cups apple cider vinegar

1/4 cup sugar

1/2 teaspoon kosher salt

1 bay leaf

1 small dried chile pepper

1 medium red onion, sliced

Combine the vinegar, sugar, salt, bay leaf, and chile pepper in a medium saucepan and bring to a boil. Stir the vinegar mixture until the sugar is dissolved, then add the onion and reduce the heat to a simmer. Cook for 5 minutes, until the onion is softened. Turn off the heat and cool the contents in the saucepan. To store, transfer to a mason jar and refrigerate for up to 1 month.

INGREDIENT NOTE

Pickled red onions will last a month in the refrigerator. Chop them up and add to various recipes that need a kick, such as green salads, grains, or sauces.

ASIAN-STYLE TUNA BURGERS WITH PICKLED GINGER MAYO AND NAPA CABBAGE SLAW

Makes 4 burgers

Prep time: 20 minutes
Cook time: 10 minutes

Here's my Asian twist on an American classic: the hamburger. After I transform tuna steaks into a ground-beef consistency in the food processor, I make them into the lightest and leanest patties you can imagine and sear them for just a few minutes on each side. A quality tuna burger like this calls for some fancy fixin's that'll make plain old pickles and mayo blush. I garnish mine with cucumbers to give texture and crunch. Southerners love their mayonnaise; here I get the best of both worlds by seasoning it with my favorite Asian flavors—ginger, soy sauce, and Sriracha hot chili sauce. The Napa Cabbage Slaw is a fresh, cool complement to the tuna burger whether you put it on the side or under the bun. Altogether, the Asian burger, sauce and side make for a triple threat.

1½ pounds tuna steaks
1 tablespoon fresh ginger, minced
2 cloves garlic, minced
1 green onion, minced
1 teaspoon toasted sesame oil
kosher salt and freshly ground black pepper
1 tablespoon canola oil
Pickled Ginger Mayo (recipe opposite)
4 soft hamburger-style buns, toasted
cucumber slices for serving
Napa Cabbage Slaw (recipe opposite)

Cut the tuna into 1-inch cubes. Add half to the bowl of a food processor and pulse about twelve times, or until finely chopped; being careful not to overprocess it. Scrape the tuna into a mixing bowl and repeat with the remaining tuna. Fold the ginger, garlic, green onion, and sesame oil into the tuna, and season with salt and pepper. Form into four equal-sized patties, about 4 inches in diameter. Transfer the patties to a plate, cover with plastic wrap, and refrigerate for about 20 minutes to firm them up.

Heat the canola oil in a nonstick pan over medium heat. Add the burgers to the hot pan and cook for just 3 minutes on each side. Spread Pickled Ginger Mayo on each toasted bun, add a tuna burger, top with cucumber slices, and sandwich between the buns. Serve with the Napa Cabbage Slaw—either on top of the patty or alongside.

INGREDIENT NOTE

We're only using a small amount of Sriracha and jalapeño here, but if your kids are adverse to any kind of heat, just leave them out.

COOKING TIP

If you're feeling lazy, you can save yourself some knife work by pulsing the ginger, garlic, and green onions in a food processor; transfer it to the mixing bowl before adding the tuna. A food processor is a busy cook's friend.

PICKLED GINGER MAYO
Makes about ½ cup

Prep time: 5 minutes   Cook time: zero

½ cup mayonnaise

2 tablespoons finely chopped pickled ginger

1 teaspoon Sriracha sauce

½ teaspoon soy sauce

Combine all your ingredients in a small bowl. The mayo can be made up to 3 days ahead. Store in the refrigerator in a tightly covered container.

NAPA CABBAGE SLAW
Makes about 3 cups

Prep time: 20 minutes   Cook time: zero

2 tablespoons lime juice

1 tablespoon rice wine vinegar

1 tablespoon sesame oil

1 tablespoon canola oil

1 teaspoon sugar

½ head Napa cabbage, shredded (about 2 cups)

1 red bell pepper, thinly sliced into matchsticks

1 carrot, well scrubbed and grated

2 green onions, thinly sliced

½ small jalapeño, seeded and thinly sliced (optional)

kosher salt

In a mixing bowl, whisk together the lime juice, rice wine vinegar, sesame oil, canola oil, and sugar. Add the cabbage, bell pepper, carrot, green onions, and jalapeño, if using, and toss all together. Season with a big pinch of salt.

Sriracha, or "the red rooster" as we call it, is a staple in my house. It goes on everything, including my chicken salad.

LAZY-DAY PULLED PORK SANDWICHES WITH SLAW

Serves 6 to 8

Prep time: 10 minutes (plus overnight marinatin')
Cook time: 5 to 7 hours

If I have the opportunity to really mess around when making dinner, I like to smoke my pork butts. But if I'm really busy, I pull out the slow cooker. I can get the pork cooking in the morning, and seven hours later, I come home and it's done. It's a delicious way to enjoy a traditional-tasting pulled pork sandwich on busy weeknights. No matter how I prepare it, I eat pulled pork the same way every time—with a big scoop of coleslaw on top. This recipe is for a coleslaw that's always been in our family; it's my favorite version because I leave out what I don't like—mainly bell peppers. I also like my coleslaw a little sweeter, so I put in some sugar and apple cider vinegar to balance out the bite of the onion and cabbage. It's not super-creamy, but it doesn't need to be—the barbecue sauce takes care of that. This simply gives you another dimension of flavor and texture to a sandwich that, by nature, is blessed.

SPICE RUB

2 tablespoons kosher salt

2 tablespoons light brown sugar

1 tablespoon paprika

1 teaspoon smoked paprika

1 teaspoon garlic powder

1/2 teaspoon ground cumin

1/2 teaspoon chili powder

1/2 teaspoon celery seed

4 pounds Boston pork butt

Jamie's Tangy BBQ Sauce (page 92)

kosher salt

6 to 8 buns

Creamy Tangy Coleslaw (recipe follows)

The night before you want to make your sandwiches, mix together all the rub ingredients in a small bowl. Rub the spice mixture on to cover the entire pork butt, including all the nooks and crannies. Place the pork on a large plate, cover with plastic wrap, and refrigerate overnight so all the flavors blend together and really infiltrate the pork.

The next morning, transfer the pork to a slow cooker and add 1 cup of BBQ sauce. Cover with the lid and cook on low heat for 7 hours, or high heat for 5 hours, until the pork is extremely tender.

Remove the pork from the slow cooker, leaving the cooking liquid behind, and place in a large bowl. Shred the pork with tongs or two forks. Drizzle in 1/4 cup of the BBQ sauce, sprinkle with a big pinch of salt, and toss it all together. Serve the pulled pork on buns, topped with the coleslaw and additional barbecue sauce.

COOKING TIP

Both the pork and the slaw taste a whole lot better if you leave them to marinate overnight.

INGREDIENT NOTE

Boston butt is a great cut of meat from the shoulder of a hog. It's generally inexpensive, serves a ton of people, and if cooked correctly, always juicy, tender, and melt-in-your-mouth delicious.

If I'm not feeling the bread, I'll just put baked beans in a bowl, layer on the pulled pork and coleslaw, and eat it all together like it's a barbeque cocktail . . . if it were in a much smaller container.

CREAMY TANGY COLESLAW
Serves 6 to 8

Prep time: 15 minutes (plus 1 hour marinatin')
Cook time: zero

1 small head (2 pounds) green cabbage, thinly sliced (about 10 cups)

1 large carrot, peeled and shredded

3 tablespoons finely chopped red onion

$^1/_2$ cup plus 1 tablespoon mayonnaise

3 tablespoons apple cider vinegar

1 tablespoon sugar

2 teaspoons yellow mustard

1 teaspoon celery seeds

kosher salt and freshly ground black pepper

Simply toss all of the ingredients together in a medium bowl, cover with plastic wrap, and let marinate in the fridge for at least 1 hour or overnight before serving.

CHICKEN SANDWICH WITH BACON, SWISS, AND CHUNKY GUACAMOLE ON GRILLED BREAD

Makes 2 sandwiches

Prep time: 10 minutes
Cook time: 20 minutes

This is a brilliant way to use up leftover roasted chicken.

This is Brooke's all-time favorite sandwich at Uncle Bubba's Oyster House, so we do it on the grill at home a lot. I've found that adding bacon and guacamole transforms a "ho-hum" chicken sandwich into something you'll have dreams about. We use avocados a lot because the boys love 'em. In fact, I've found that they will roll their sleeves up for anything I put guacamole on—it's kind of like how you can get a dog to take a pill by hiding it in a cube of cheese.

4 slices bacon

4 slices nice crusty sourdough bread

4 tablespoons butter, at room temperature

1 cup cooked chicken, roughly chopped

4 deli slices Swiss cheese

1/2 beefsteak tomato, thinly sliced

CHUNKY GUACAMOLE

1 large ripe avocado, pitted and diced

3 tablespoons minced red onion

1 tablespoon sour cream

1 tablespoon lime juice (about half a lime)

kosher salt

Preheat the oven to 400°F.

Place the bacon on a foil-lined sheet tray and bake for 10 to 12 minutes, or until crisp. Transfer to a paper towel–lined plate to drain.

Meanwhile, make the guacamole: In a mixing bowl, coarsely mash the avocado, onion, sour cream, and lime juice. Season with a big pinch of salt and set aside.

Heat a grill pan over medium-high heat. Spread both sides of the bread slices with the butter and grill until crisp and golden grill marks appear, about 2 minutes per side. Divide the chicken between two slices of the bread, then layer each with the bacon and Swiss cheese. Return the sandwiches to the grill pan and cover with a domed lid just until the cheese is melted, 1 to 2 minutes. Carefully remove the lid and remove the sandwiches from the grill.

Top your sandwiches with the tomato slices. Spread the remaining two slices of bread with the chunky guacamole and close up each sandwich. Slice them in half for serving.

INGREDIENT NOTE

Guacamole is a great alternative to mayonnaise. It has the same satisfyingly creamy texture but it's colorful and good for you. In this version, keeping it a little chunky makes it seem even more filling—plus, I don't like to skimp. This recipe makes about 3/4 cup, enough for several sandwiches.

THE FOUR PILLARS

In 1989, my mom called me up to tell me that she was starting a business and needed my help. She was going to sell sack lunches. I pictured her wandering into school cafeterias, finding the kids whose mommas couldn't find their way around a kitchen, and selling them a sandwich for 50 cents—not exactly the road to riches. I wasn't too far off. In the beginning, Mom would get up before the sun and make around fifty sandwiches. At lunchtime, she wanted me to drive them over to the Medical Arts Building where she had worked. There, I'd sell sack lunches to her friends, who preferred the home-cooked taste of Mom's sandwiches to the bag of chips stuffed in their desk drawers that they often scarfed down between appointments.

She didn't ask for help, she *told* me I was going to help. Reluctantly, I showed up to work, not because I was excited about the venture (I wasn't), but because I didn't have much else going on. I had finished college and was let loose into the world without any real sense of where I was headed, so home seemed like as good a prospect as any. At least I was guaranteed a meal, which was better than the majority of my college days.

I was as charismatic as any twenty-something, basket-carrying, sandwich-peddling kid could be, but Mom's business was really built around four pillars: pimento cheese (see Bits and Pieces, page 207, for my perfected take on this recipe), chicken, tuna, and egg salad sandwiches.

I had grown up on those lunches, so at first I didn't realize what all the fuss was about. Eventually I realized what I'd taken for granted all those years—Mom could really cook.

Momma didn't do anything fancy. She made honest, straightforward meals that people liked. That people were willing to pay for. It was the most basic equation. And as much as I resented her business at the time, it taught me the value of simple food, made well, which is why my first solo cookbook—and my life—wouldn't be the same without the Four Pillars, presented here as I like to serve them. But feel free to sandwich them between slices of your favorite bread.

EGG SALAD
Serves 4

Prep time: 10 minutes
Cook time: zero

In Louisiana, they refer to onion, pepper, and celery as the "Holy Trinity"; that's the cook-down basis for every gumbo, jambalaya, or *grillade* that they make. But in Georgia, the Holy Trinity is chicken salad, tuna salad, and egg salad—with egg salad as the daddy of them all. And here again you'll see that I've managed to sneak bacon into my egg salad recipe to give it a salty, savory, divine finish. So please, show some respect.

6 hard-boiled eggs, peeled and
coarsely chopped (see Cooking Tip)

4 slices bacon, cooked crisp and crumbled

1/3 cup mayonnaise

1/4 cup dill pickle relish

1 tablespoon roughly chopped fresh dill

1 teaspoon Dijon mustard

kosher salt and freshly ground black pepper

celery sticks for serving (optional)

In a medium bowl, mix together the eggs, bacon, mayonnaise, relish, dill, Dijon, and salt and pepper. Serve with celery sticks, if you like.

COOKING TIP

The answer to the egg-peeling conundrum: Cook your eggs in water seasoned with a bunch of salt. As soon as the water boils, cover the pot and turn off the heat; let it sit for 10 minutes and your eggs are done. Peel them under running water. Now go forward and prosper, young Jedi.

TUNA SALAD

Serves 4

Prep time: 5 minutes
Cook time: zero

Tuna salad on soda crackers is one of my favorite snacks. You won't even dirty a fork.

Layers of flavor from the onion, lemon juice, and sweet pickle relish transform your run-of-the-mill tuna-and-mayo combination into something special. Look back to the Egg Salad recipe for my perfect egg-peeling method.

2 cans (6 ounces each) solid white tuna packed in water, drained

2 hard-boiled eggs, peeled and finely chopped

1/3 cup mayonnaise

juice of half a lemon

3 tablespoons thinly sliced chives

1 stalk celery, finely chopped

1 tablespoon sweet pickle relish

1 tablespoon finely chopped red onion

kosher salt and freshly ground black pepper

mixed salad greens (optional)

toasted sourdough or whole-wheat bread (optional)

In a mixing bowl, combine the tuna, eggs, mayonnaise, lemon juice, chives, celery, relish, and onion. Season the salad with a big pinch of salt and pepper and stir to combine. Serve on a bed of salad greens or on toasted bread, if you like.

CHICKEN SALAD

Serves 6

Prep time: 10 minutes
Cook time: zero

Chicken Salad is something we've made our whole lives. It was one of the "trio salads" we made religiously at The Bag Lady. But for our "high-end" items on Fridays, we'd grill the chicken for the salad. Or, rather, Dad would. He'd go out at like 5 o'clock in the morning to grill the chicken and later we'd pick that poultry clean. Grilled chicken salad sandwiches would fly out of our hands at a whopping $5 a pop. That's a whole lot of sandwiches when you consider how far we've come since The Bag Lady.

1/3 cup mayonnaise

1 tablespoon lemon juice

3 green onions, finely chopped

kosher salt and freshly ground black pepper

3 cups cooked and chopped chicken

1 cup red seedless grapes, sliced in half

1/2 cup chopped and toasted walnuts

6 beefsteak tomatoes for serving (optional)

In a medium bowl, whisk together the mayonnaise, lemon juice, green onions, and salt and pepper, then fold in the chicken, grapes, and walnuts. Taste and adjust the seasoning.

To serve in the tomatoes, slice off the tops. Use a paring knife to cut around the inside of the tomatoes, then use a spoon to scoop out the pulp and discard it. Season with salt and pepper, then fill with the chicken salad for serving.

COOKING TIP

We love to serve this salad in a hollowed-out tomato for an interesting presentation—and that's one less bowl to clean.

BY LAND

By Land

I've never been a hunter. Growing up, I think I saw *Bambi* one too many times to ever be able to shoot a deer—or any creature for that matter. Dad took Bobby and me bird hunting back when I was in the fifth or sixth grade. It was fun at first—tracking the birds, sneaking up on 'em, and taking aim. But what came after didn't sit so well with either one of us. The Deen boys didn't have the heart for hunting—or maybe we had too much heart to ever enjoy it.

The truth is, I've always felt that if you do hunt, you should eat what you shoot, and I don't eat game enough to justify hunting it. Today I enjoy shooting skeet out at this beautiful, private gun club in Savannah—one of the oldest in the country. Wednesday is "Men's Night" and it's probably the busiest time of the week. Nobody gets hurt except a flying clay disk, and, after a few high-fives with my buddies, I can head home to a roast chicken with a big appetite and a clear conscience.

We were fortunate that beef, chicken, and pork were always a staple on our table when I was growing up. But don't feel as if you're limited by just three kinds of meat. Each one is available in so many different cuts. When it comes to chicken, there are legs, thighs, wings, and breast meat. Some red meat is more marbled; some has less fat. There are just as many different cuts of pork: You can get a pork chop, tenderloin, or ribs, just to name a few. The point is, if you take the time to learn about the different cuts, you'll discover a wide variety of distinct textures, flavors, and possible preparations to keep you from getting stuck in a rut.

I still cook meat most days of the week, but it's less about quantity now—no more elbowing my brother out to get the last rib—and more about the quality of the preparation and presentation. Certain dishes, like a savory roast beef tenderloin or a sweet and salty maple-glazed ham, can pretty much stand on their own, but I like to play with flavor pairing. The addition of white wine and leeks to One-Pot Chicken and Rice blows the lid off this traditional dish, in much the same way that a sausage-and-herb stuffing cranks up the appeal of an already delicious pork tenderloin. But nothing in this chapter outshines Brooke's Meatloaf. Now *that* I'm willing to bet Bambi's life on.

SUNDAY ROAST CHICKEN WITH SEASONAL VEGETABLES

Serves 4

Prep time: 15 minutes
Cook time: 1 hour 10 minutes

I use my Granny Paul's skillet for this dish. It becomes more seasoned every time I use it, making it the most seasoned skillet in the history of humankind.

Sundays are the only day of the week when my family doesn't have a full slate of errands and events: No school, soccer games, or birthday parties in bouncy houses that'll inevitably lead to an emergency-room visit. That means I'm able to plan and prepare this favorite family meal. A roast chicken falls right in line with relaxed Sundays—even though it takes a while to cook, it's not labor-intensive and it's a beautiful dish that's both affordable and healthful. The preparation is always the same, but I change out the vegetables with the season. Whichever vegetables you prefer, the essence from the chicken seasons them all to create one delicious dish.

COOKING TIP

Save the leftover chicken carcass for Homemade Chicken Stock (page 205).

Take the chicken out of the refrigerator, remove the innards from the cavity, and pat it dry with paper towels. Let the chicken stand at room temperature for about 1 hour.

Mince the leaves of 1 sprig of rosemary. In a small bowl, mix together the butter, minced rosemary, and garlic. Rub the chicken with the herb butter, making sure to spread some under the skin. Season the cavity of the chicken with salt and pepper, and add 1 sprig of rosemary. Liberally season the buttery outside of the chicken with salt and pepper.

Preheat the oven to 475°F and adjust the rack to the center of the oven.

In a large roasting pan or ovenproof skillet, toss your vegetables and remaining rosemary sprig with the oil, and season with salt and pepper. Make sure the vegetables are well coated with the oil—they should look glossy.

Place a roasting rack over the vegetables and put the chicken on the rack, or just lay the chicken over the veggies. Roast for 20 minutes until the skin is nice and browned, then knock down the heat to 400°F and roast for another 50 to 75 minutes, depending on if the chicken is on a rack or on the veggies, until a thermometer inserted into the thickest part of the thigh reads 165°F, and the juices run nice and clear. Transfer the chicken to a cutting board, and let rest for 15 minutes.

Meanwhile, using a slotted spoon, transfer the vegetables to a serving bowl. Cover them loosely with foil to keep warm. Place the roasting pan on two burners over medium heat. Add the stock and use a wooden spoon to scrape up the delicious browned bits on the bottom of the pan. Reduce the liquid by about half, or until the pan juices coat the back of a spoon. Be sure to add any of the juices that may have accumulated from the resting chicken.

Carve the chicken and serve with the roasted vegetables and the pan juices.

1 chicken (4 pounds)

3 sprigs fresh rosemary

3 tablespoons butter, at room temperature

1 clove garlic, minced

kosher salt and freshly ground black pepper

seasonal vegetables (see Ingredient Notes)

3 tablespoons olive oil

1/2 cup Homemade Chicken Stock (page 205)

INGREDIENT NOTES

I always use a variety of vegetables with roasted
chicken based on what's fresh and in season.
Here are some suggestions:

FALL/WINTER

1 russet potato (12 ounces), well scrubbed and
cut into 1½-inch cubes

1 sweet potato (12 ounces), peeled and cut into
1½-inch cubes

2 rutabagas, peeled and cut into 1-inch cubes

2 parsnips, well scrubbed and cut into
1-inch pieces

1 large red onion, cut into 6 wedges

SPRING

1 pound fingerling potatoes, sliced in half

1 bunch English radishes, well scrubbed,
tops removed

2 large leeks, dark green tops and outer layer
removed, sliced in half lengthwise just below
the root

2 medium carrots, well scrubbed and sliced into
1-inch pieces (thick ends cut in half)

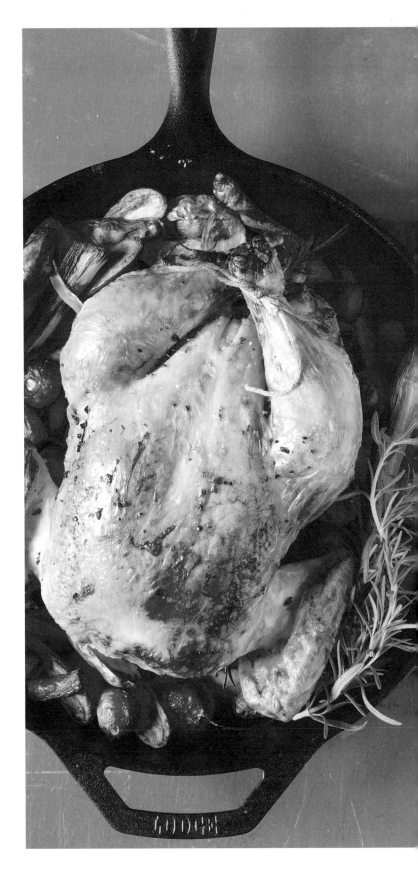

A comforting Sunday dinner never sounded so easy . . . or tasted so good.

This dish takes me way back to when Bobby and I were just boys. It's an affordable recipe, which is why Momma made it. We may not have had ski lessons or European vacations growing up, but we always had first-rate meals. Momma's dumplings were always homemade, so these are too. If you don't have the time, you can get some store-bought ones and drop 'em in, but I'm telling y'all, they're really simple to do. Everyone has their version of a dumplin'—Japan has gyoza, Italy has gnocchi, and Poland has pierogi—but it all boils down to a ball of dough. It can have a filling or special ingredients mixed into the dough, but I like my dumplings plain and simple: flour, salt, and water.

MOMMA'S CHICKEN AND DUMPLINGS

Serves 6

Prep time: 30 minutes
Cook time: 1 hour 20 minutes

In a large Dutch oven, combine the chicken, onion, celery, carrots, thyme, bay leaves, salt, and peppercorns. Cover with the cold water and bring to a boil. Reduce the heat to low and simmer gently for 45 minutes, or until the chicken is completely cooked through and tender.

Meanwhile, make the dumpling dough: Combine the flour and salt in a large bowl. Gradually sprinkle in the water, mixing it with your hands, until the dough comes together. Dump the dough onto a lightly floured surface and knead it together into a disk. Sprinkle the dough lightly with additional flour and roll it out to 1/8-inch thickness. Let the dough rest for 30 minutes.

When the chicken is done, transfer to a large plate to cool. Once it's cool enough to handle, shred the meat from the chicken with a fork, discarding the skin and bones. Strain the broth and discard the remaining solid pieces. Bring the broth back up to a simmer and reduce for about 10 minutes, until you have 8 cups.

Using a pizza cutter, slice the dough into 1-inch squares. Drop the squares into the simmering broth. Gently shake the Dutch oven back and forth so the dumplings don't stick together. Simmer until the dumplings are cooked through and float to the top of the broth, 5 to 6 minutes. Gently stir in the shredded chicken, reduce the heat to low, and simmer for 15 to 20 minutes more, until the soup thickens.

1 chicken (3 1/2 pounds), quartered

1 large onion, roughly chopped

4 stalks celery, roughly chopped, plus the leaves for serving

2 carrots, roughly chopped

8 sprigs fresh thyme

2 bay leaves

1 tablespoon kosher salt

1 teaspoon black peppercorns

10 cups cold water

DUMPLINGS

2 cups all-purpose flour, plus more for dusting

1 teaspoon kosher salt

3/4 cup cold water

COOKING TIP

Although Mom may not reduce her broth, I've found it's a surefire way to amp up the flavor. But I'm not gonna tell her that.

CRISPY PARMESAN CHICKEN CUTLETS WITH ARUGULA AND AVOCADO

Serves 4

Prep time: 15 minutes
Cook time: 15 minutes

Let's not kid ourselves; sometimes one cutlet just won't cut it. In that case, double down.

Universally speaking, most kids love chicken nuggets and our boys are no exception. That said, Brooke and I just can't get behind processed deep-fried-then-frozen nuggets, let alone the kind that come in unnatural shapes. I'm good with pasta being formed into wheels or letters, but dinosaur-shaped nuggets? Not so much. We've found that cooking chicken cutlets on the stovetop with a bit of oil after dredging them with Parmesan and panko—a Japanese-style of breading that's lighter and crispier than a thick batter—produces a fresh and delicious alternative to processed prehistoric nuggets. Here we serve them on a bed of baby arugula, along with slices of creamy avocado, which is also a big hit in our house.

2 boneless, skinless chicken breasts (9 ounces each)

kosher salt and freshly ground black pepper

$1/2$ cup all-purpose flour

2 large eggs, beaten

$1\frac{1}{4}$ cups panko breadcrumbs

$1/3$ cup finely grated Parmesan cheese

1 teaspoon lemon zest

$2/3$ cup canola oil

5 ounces baby arugula

1 large ripe avocado, pitted and sliced into wedges

juice of $1/2$ lemon (about 2 tablespoons)

1 tablespoon olive oil

lemon wedges for serving

Lay the chicken breasts out on a cutting board. Hold your knife parallel to the cutting board and slice a breast in half, so one breast is now two cutlets. Repeat with the second breast. Lay the cutlets between two sheets of plastic wrap and pound with a meat mallet to ¼-inch thickness. Season the cutlets on both sides with salt and pepper.

Arrange three plates in front of you. Add the flour to the first and the beaten eggs to the second. Combine the panko, Parmesan, lemon zest, and salt and pepper in the third.

Dredge each cutlet first through the flour, then the egg, and finally the panko mixture. Arrange them on a clean sheet tray. Refrigerate for 1 hour.

Preheat the oven to 200°F.

Heat the canola oil in a large nonstick skillet over medium heat. Once it's hot, add the cutlets, in two batches, and cook until golden brown on the outside and cooked through, about 3 minutes on each side. Transfer to paper towels to drain and season with salt right when they come out of the pan. Transfer the cutlets onto a sheet tray and keep in the warm oven while you cook the second batch.

Place the arugula and avocado in a large bowl. Drizzle with the lemon juice, olive oil, and season with salt and pepper. Toss it all together really well and divide the salad between four plates. Top each salad with a cutlet, place a lemon wedge on each plate, and serve immediately.

COOKING TIP

If your child isn't a fan of arugula's unique flavor, you can opt for baby spinach or a milder lettuce.

ONE-POT CHICKEN AND RICE WITH LEEKS AND GREEN OLIVES

Serves 4

Prep time: 10 minutes
Cook time: 1 hour 5 minutes

In this fancied-up version of old-fashioned chicken and rice, I've added leeks, green olives, and white wine—ingredients more likely to appear in a fine-dining restaurant than in a weekday dish. But in this case, fancy still means affordable and satisfying because the foundation is rice and chicken thighs—which I prefer to use in this recipe because they tend to be juicier than white meat.

2 tablespoons olive oil

2 pounds boneless, skinless chicken thighs (about 8 thighs)

kosher salt and freshly ground black pepper

2 leeks, rinsed well, trimmed and sliced crosswise

4 cloves garlic, chopped

2 plum tomatoes, chopped (about $1/2$ pound)

$1/2$ cup white wine

$1/2$ cup water

1 cup long-grain white rice

$2/3$ cup green olives, pitted and coarsely chopped

$1/4$ cup chopped fresh parsley leaves for serving (optional)

Heat the oil in a large Dutch oven or heavy, high-sided skillet over medium-high heat. Season the chicken thighs on both sides with salt and pepper. Once the oil is hot, brown the chicken, in batches, for 3 minutes per side, or until golden. Transfer the chicken to a platter and set aside.

Reduce the heat to medium. Add the leeks and sauté until soft, about 5 minutes, scraping up any browned bits from the bottom of the pot once the leeks release their water.

Add the garlic and cook until fragrant, stirring, 1 to 2 minutes. Add the tomatoes and cook about 4 minutes more, stirring occasionally, until softened and the leeks and tomatoes melt into each other. Pour in the wine and water and stir to combine. Add the reserved chicken thighs and any juices that may have accumulated on the plate. Cover the pot with a lid, turn the heat to medium-low, and cook for 25 minutes.

Transfer most of the chicken to a platter, and then stir in the rice and olives, making sure the rice is completely submerged in liquid. Return the chicken to the pot, nestling the thighs into the rice and cooking liquid. Cover and cook for 30 minutes, until the rice is tender and the liquid has been absorbed, rotating the pan throughout cooking.

Turn off the heat and allow the rice to steam for 5 minutes before serving. Fluff the rice with a fork. I like to serve this in bowls, with chopped parsley on top.

COOKING TIP

Make sure you clean the leeks really well. I'll even let them soak in a bowl of ice water for a few minutes so I can be sure they're super clean. There's nothing worse than a good meal ruined by gritty leeks!

BUTTERMILK OVEN-FRIED CHICKEN

Serves 4

Prep time: 10 minutes
Cook time: 45 minutes (plus 1 hour marinatin')

Southerners know better than anyone how to fry a chicken. I don't mean to go against my raising here—because I will be the first to admit that nothing will ever replace fried chicken—but this baked version is pretty darn good. The panko, Japanese breadcrumbs that you can find at most any grocery, forms a satisfying, crispy shell around the meat, which stays perfectly moist. It's a healthier alternative and much easier to clean up—a double bonus for parents everywhere.

1 chicken (3½ pounds), cut into 8 pieces (use wings for another recipe)

2 teaspoons kosher salt

1 teaspoon freshly ground black pepper

1 teaspoon garlic powder

⅛ teaspoon ground thyme

1½ cups low-fat buttermilk

¼ cup hot sauce

2 tablespoons Dijon mustard

1 teaspoon paprika

2 cups panko breadcrumbs

2 tablespoons melted butter

Season the chicken pieces with the salt, pepper, garlic powder, and thyme. Place the chicken on a plate, cover with plastic wrap, and refrigerate for 8 hours. (If you're in a hurry, let the chicken sit at room temperature for 1 hour.)

In a large mixing bowl, whisk together the buttermilk, hot sauce, Dijon, and paprika. Add the seasoned chicken to the bowl, making sure it's fully covered with the buttermilk mixture. Cover and refrigerate for 1 hour.

Preheat the oven to 400°F. Place a rack inside a rimmed baking sheet and spray it with nonstick cooking spray.

Season the breadcrumbs with salt and pepper and whisk together in a medium baking dish. Remove the chicken pieces from the buttermilk, letting the excess drip off, then dredge them through the breadcrumbs one at a time, patting the crumbs to the chicken to adhere. Evenly space the chicken pieces on the rack and lightly drizzle with the melted butter. Bake for 45 minutes, until the chicken is cooked through and the breading is golden brown.

MAPLE-GLAZED CHRISTMAS HAM

Serves 15 to 20

Prep time: 5 minutes
Cook time: 4 1/2 hours

This Christmas ham is a tradition that my mom passed down to us and I'm happy to share it with y'all. Even after a big Christmas breakfast with Brooke's parents, I still have room for Mom's ham at dinnertime. The Dijon combined with the brown sugar and the syrup creates such a beautiful glaze and boasts an incredible flavor that plays perfectly against the ham's saltiness. The shank end is attractive on the table plus a little less fatty with more meat than the butt end. Serve with Creamy Potato Gratin (page 143) and the Fall Harvest Salad with Maple Vinaigrette (page 16).

1 cooked and smoked bone-in ham (15 pounds), preferably the shank end

MAPLE GLAZE
1/4 cup butter
1/4 cup maple syrup
1/4 cup firmly packed light brown sugar
2 teaspoons chopped fresh thyme
2 teaspoons Dijon mustard
kosher salt and freshly ground black pepper

Preheat the oven to 350°F and move a rack to the lower third of the oven.

Using a sharp knife, score a diamond pattern into the top and sides of the ham. Place a rack in the bottom of a large roasting pan and set the ham on top. Pour 1 quart water into the bottom of the pan and cover the pan tightly with foil. Bake the ham for 18 minutes per pound, for a total of 4 hours.

Meanwhile, start on the glaze: In a small saucepan over medium heat, combine the butter, maple syrup, brown sugar, thyme, and Dijon. Season with salt and pepper to taste and simmer, while stirring frequently, for 4 to 5 minutes. Set the glaze aside as the ham bakes.

After 4 hours, remove the foil from the ham and glaze it every 5 minutes for 30 minutes. Once the internal temperature reaches 148°F, the ham is heated through. Remove the ham from the oven and let stand for 10 minutes. Brush again with the glaze and carve.

COOKING TIP

Use the "buddy method." Pass time in the kitchen chatting with a friend since you're going to be anchored to the oven, glazing the ham every 5 minutes, for the last half hour of cooking.

ROAST PORK LOIN WITH SAUSAGE, FIGS, AND FRESH HERBS

Serves 6

Prep time: 15 minutes
Cook time: 1 hour 5 minutes

We make this recipe a lot at home. It has the "I slaved in the kitchen all day" look, but really takes no time at all. If you're looking for a memorable celebratory meal, the layers of flavor wrapped into this pork loin make this a surefire bet. Just be sure to have copies of the recipe to share with your guests; I guarantee they'll ask. We served it up here with some sautéed baby kale.

1 tablespoon olive oil

1 pound Italian sausage, casings removed

3 cloves garlic, chopped

4 large fresh sage leaves, rubbed

1 tablespoon chopped fresh rosemary

1 tablespoon chopped fresh thyme

kosher salt and freshly ground black pepper

1 cup finely chopped dried figs

1/4 cup dry white wine

3 tablespoons chopped fresh parsley

1 boneless center-cut pork loin (3 pounds)

RUB

2 tablespoons olive oil

1 1/2 teaspoons fennel seeds

1 tablespoon roughly chopped fresh rosemary

kosher salt and freshly ground black pepper

Preheat the oven to 425°F. Line your sheet tray with a piece of foil.

Heat the olive oil in a large skillet over medium-high heat. Once it's hot, add the sausage meat and cook until browned, stirring and breaking it up with the back of a wooden spoon, about 4 minutes. Stir in the garlic, sage, rosemary, and thyme, season with salt and pepper, then cook for 2 minutes more, until fragrant. Stir in the figs, sauté for 1 minute more, then hit it with the white wine. Scrape up any browned bits that form on the bottom of the pan and cook until the stuffing is almost dry, about 3 minutes. Transfer to a bowl, stir in the parsley, and let cool completely.

Next, butterfly your roast: Take a sharp knife and cut down through the center of the loin, opening it up like a book (leave two inches on one end, being sure not to cut all the way through). Pound the pork with a meat mallet until it's an even 1 1/2-inch thickness. Season with salt and pepper. Spoon the cooled stuffing mixture down the center of the roast, and roll it up like a jelly roll into a tight cylinder. Tie the pork loin every 2 inches with kitchen string. Transfer the tied roast onto the foil-lined sheet tray.

To prepare the rub, place the olive oil, fennel seeds, rosemary, and salt and pepper to taste in a mortar and grind with a pestle into a paste (you could also use a spice grinder or a coffee grinder used just for spices).

Rub the outside of the pork with the paste and season again with salt and pepper. Lay the pork, fat side up, on the sheet tray and roast for 30 minutes. Lower the heat to 350°F and continue to roast for another 25 minutes, until a meat thermometer inserted into the thickest part of the meat reads 145°F. Let the pork loin rest for 15 minutes before slicing and serving.

Turn the page to see how to stuff and tie up the loin . . .

People are always impressed when you bother to stuff a pork loin, but really, it's just a dressed-up version of a pig in the blanket. Okay, make that a really dressed-up version.

GRILLED PORK CHOPS WITH HONEY-ORANGE MUSTARD GLAZE

Serves 4

Prep time: 5 minutes
Cook time: 20 minutes

Because Brooke and I don't fry food in our home kitchen, I've started grilling my pork chops, but they have a tendency to dry out. So I came up with a really good glaze that incorporates sweet, citrus, and savory flavors and seals in the moisture, too. It's a simple summertime supper that takes less than 30 minutes, start-to-finish. These pork chops are awesome with the Greek Salad Couscous (page 147) or the Grilled Rainbow Chopped Salad (page 24).

$\frac{1}{3}$ cup orange juice

2 tablespoons honey

2 tablespoons Dijon mustard

1 tablespoon soy sauce

4 bone-in center-cut pork chops (each 1 inch thick)

kosher salt and freshly ground black pepper

Heat an outdoor grill to medium-high.

In a small saucepan, whisk together the orange juice, honey, Dijon, and soy sauce. Reduce the sauce over medium heat until it's thick like maple syrup, about 7 minutes.

Season the pork chops on both sides with salt and pepper. Grill the chops for 5 minutes on each side, brushing both sides with the glaze during the last 2 minutes of cooking, and again just before taking them off the grill.

BROOKE'S MEATLOAF WITH SUN-DRIED TOMATOES AND FRESH MOZZARELLA

Serves 8

Prep time: 10 minutes
Cook time: 1 hour

Hands down, my wife's meatloaf is the best thing I've ever eaten in my life.

Brooke doesn't cook much, but when she cooks this, buddy, look out. I'll have her meatloaf for dinner and then I'll make a meatloaf sandwich for dessert. Honest to God. Brooke prefers to use sun-dried tomatoes jarred in olive oil because they're moist and flavorful. The fresh breadcrumbs add lightness, too.

1 medium onion, finely chopped

2 cloves garlic, minced

2 large eggs, lightly beaten

$1/2$ cup chopped sun-dried tomatoes, drained from oil

1 cup fresh breadcrumbs (see Ingredient Note)

1 ball fresh mozzarella (8 ounces), finely chopped

$1 1/4$ cups Basic Tomato Sauce (page 206)

$1/4$ cup chopped fresh basil

kosher salt and freshly ground black pepper

2 pounds lean ground beef

Preheat the oven to 350°F. Line a sheet tray with foil.

To a large mixing bowl, add the onion, garlic, eggs, sun-dried tomatoes, breadcrumbs, mozzarella, $1/4$ cup of the tomato sauce, and basil and give it a good stir to combine. Season the mixture with a generous pinch of salt and pepper. Add the beef, season with another pinch of salt and pepper, and toss it all together with your hands, just until combined. (Be sure not to overdo it or the meatloaf will be dense and heavy rather than nice and light.)

Plop the beef down on the prepared sheet tray and use your hands to form it into a loaf shape. Drizzle the top with $3/4$ cup of the remaining tomato sauce and bake for 55 minutes. Drizzle the remaining $1/4$ cup tomato sauce on top and cook for 5 minutes more, for a total of 1 hour.

Remove the meatloaf from the oven and let it rest for 10 minutes before slicing it up and serving.

INGREDIENT NOTE

It's important to use fresh breadcrumbs here. To make them, add a 4-ounce chunk of baguette to a food processor and grind it up until it's a fine texture.

JACK'S PORCUPINES

Serves 4 to 6

Prep time: 10 minutes
Cook time: 55 minutes

This is a cute recipe that you can do for the kids, and the parents will like it as well because it's really satisfying. Basically, it's a jacked-up meatball. Bobby and I got a big kick out of it when we were growing up and I'm sure it'll make its way into your rotation of weekday go-to meals as well.

1 pound lean ground beef

1¹/₂ cups long-grain white rice

¹/₂ cup finely grated Parmesan cheese

1 small onion, finely diced

2 cloves garlic, minced

kosher salt and freshly ground black pepper

1 can (14¹/₂ ounces) fire-roasted diced tomatoes

2 cups low-sodium or Homemade Chicken Stock (page 205)

Preheat the oven to 350°F. Spray a 13 by 9-inch baking dish with nonstick cooking spray.

In a large mixing bowl, gently combine the ground beef, ¹/₂ cup of the rice, Parmesan, half of the onion, and the garlic and season with a big pinch of salt and pepper. Roll the mixture into twelve golf ball–size meatballs.

In the prepared baking dish, place the remaining 1 cup rice, the tomatoes with their juices, stock, and remaining onion. Season with salt and pepper and stir to combine. Add the meatballs to the dish, turning to coat them with the liquid. Cover the dish with foil and bake for 55 minutes.

Remove the foil from the top of the baking dish and admire your cute little porcupine meatballs! Serve the meatballs over the tomato rice.

RED WINE–BRAISED SHORT RIBS WITH HERBED RICE PILAF

Serves 6 (about 8 ribs per serving)

Prep time: 20 minutes
Cook time: 3 1/2 hours

Scraping browned bits is the cooking version of panning for gold. It's the way to get the most concentrated flavor you can out of a dish.

Ribs are not a "first date" kind of food. To get at the meat, you've got to be willing to throw yourself into it, elbows and all. Luckily, once you're married, you no longer have to suffer through awkward dinners using a tiny fork while being strangled by an overly starched shirt. You can scratch, wear comfy pants, and eat ribs with abandon. My boys already understand this—they've grown up cutting their teeth on rib bones. That's where the flavor is. I know it's common advice to select a cut of meat that's marbled with fat because it offers a lot of flavor, but that's not the case here. Because it's a bone-in rib, there's already going to be a lot of flavor even before you sauce it up.

This recipe is also a snap to make because most of the work can be done in advance, giving you a couple of hours to enjoy that little bit of after-school time you have with the family while your ribs are cooking. And the process is even more enjoyable if you take a cue I learned from Justin Wilson, the first television chef I ever watched: Every time he poured wine into a recipe, he'd take a nip—sometimes straight from the bottle. Which leads me to another important point: You don't need a top-tier wine to cook with, nor do you want a bottom-of-the-barrel brand. Always cook with what you enjoy drinking. What's left in the bottle makes for a nice pairing and a romantic gesture—and helps my wife overlook the comfy pants.

5 pounds meaty short ribs, trimmed of excess fat

kosher salt and freshly ground black pepper

4 tablespoons olive oil

1 red onion, finely chopped

2 stalks celery, finely chopped

1 carrot, peeled and finely chopped

3 cloves garlic, peeled and smashed

2 tablespoons chopped fresh rosemary

2 tablespoons tomato paste

2 1/2 cups dry red wine

2 1/2 to 3 cups low-sodium or Homemade Chicken Stock (page 205)

1 bunch fresh thyme

1 dried bay leaf

chopped fresh parsley for serving

Preheat the oven to 325°F.

Pat the short ribs dry and season them up good on both sides with salt and pepper. Heat 2 tablespoons oil in a large Dutch oven over medium-high heat. Once the oil is hot, add the short ribs, in two batches, and brown 'em really well on all sides. Each batch should take a good 15 minutes to get that nice dark brown color. (Be patient 'cause that color means flavor.) Remove the first batch of browned short ribs to a platter and repeat with the second batch.

Drain off the fat from the pot, add the remaining 2 tablespoons oil, and return to medium-high heat. Once it's hot—and it shouldn't take long—add the onion, carrots, celery, and garlic and sauté until softened and browned, about 6 minutes. Season with salt and pepper and add the rosemary. Stir in the tomato paste and brown for 3 minutes, stirring. Add the wine and 2½ cups stock to the pot, and scrape up any delicious browned bits from the bottom of the pot with the back of your wooden spoon. There's lots of flavor here, so be sure to get it into the sauce. Bring the mixture up to a simmer and return the ribs to the pot, making sure they are just covered with liquid, adding a bit more stock, if you need to. Tie the thyme and bay leaf together using kitchen twine and drop it right into the pot.

Cover the inside lid of the pot with some foil and put the lid on the pot. Place the pot in the oven for 2½ hours, until the ribs are super tender and the meat is about to fall off the

bone. Remove the ribs to a baking dish, discarding bones if they fall off, and cover with the foil from the top of the lid to keep warm.

Place the Dutch oven over medium heat on the stovetop and reduce the sauce for about 10 minutes, until it's thick enough to lightly coat the back of a spoon.

Serve the short ribs over a bed of Herbed Rice Pilaf (page 90). Sprinkle with the parsley.

INGREDIENT NOTES

When shopping for short ribs, look for the meatiest ribs with the least visible fat. I like the flanken cut, which is sliced across the bones.

If you opt for a store-bought broth to save time, you'll want to get the low-sodium version. The liquid will reduce throughout the long cooking process, intensifying the salty flavor.

COOKING TIP

This is a fantastic dish for entertaining because all the work is done ahead of time. Just take the short ribs out of the pot and reduce the sauce right before your guests are ready to eat.

HERBED RICE PILAF

Short ribs are so rich that it's wise to pair them with this herbed rice pilaf. The rice offers a nice, bright contrast to the heavy sauce and meat. The combo may sound fancy, but kids love ribs and rice.

Serves 6

Prep time: 10 minutes
Cook time: 25 minutes

2 tablespoons butter

1 small onion, finely chopped

1 clove garlic, peeled and smashed

kosher salt and freshly ground black pepper

1 dried bay leaf

3 sprigs fresh thyme

1$\frac{1}{2}$ cups long-grain white rice

2$\frac{1}{2}$ cups Homemade Chicken Stock (page 205)

3 tablespoons roughly chopped fresh parsley

In a medium saucepan, melt the butter over medium heat. Add the onion and garlic and season with salt and pepper. Cook, stirring occasionally, until the onion is softened, about 5 minutes. Stir in the bay leaf and thyme during the last minute of sautéing. Add the rice and stir to coat with the butter. Pour in the stock, bring to a boil, reduce the heat to a simmer, and cook, covered, until the rice is tender, 15 to 17 minutes. Let stand for 5 minutes, then fluff with a fork and fold in the parsley.

INGREDIENT NOTE

Using chicken stock rather than water takes this rice up a notch. The fresh parsley gives it a little kick of color, too. If your child's afraid of all things green, skip this step.

ROAST BEEF TENDERLOIN WITH ROSEMARY

Serves 6

Prep time: 15 minutes
Cook time: 25 minutes

I don't know how many people still put out two kinds of meat at Christmas dinner, but Momma has been doing this beef tenderloin alongside a ham for as long as I can remember. Even on its own, this no-fuss roast is always a showstopper—you're not gonna serve this if you've got the paper plates out.

5 tablespoons olive oil

2 cloves garlic

3 tablespoons chopped fresh rosemary, plus 2 sprigs rosemary

kosher salt and freshly ground black pepper

2$\frac{1}{2}$ pounds beef tenderloin roast, tied with kitchen string at every 1 inch

CREAMY HORSERADISH SAUCE
(MAKES ABOUT 1 CUP)

1 cup sour cream

2$\frac{1}{2}$ tablespoons prepared horseradish

2 tablespoons heavy cream

1 small shallot, minced

2 teaspoons Dijon mustard

kosher salt and freshly ground black pepper

To the bowl of a food processor, add 3 tablespoons of the olive oil, the garlic, chopped rosemary, and a big pinch of salt and pepper and puree until you have a nice paste. Rub the entire roast with the puree, making sure to get into every nook and cranny. Let the roast sit for 1 hour at room temperature to take off the chill and let the flavors marry.

Meanwhile, make the creamy horseradish sauce: In a small bowl, mix together the sour cream, horseradish, heavy cream, shallot, and Dijon, and season with salt and pepper. Cover with plastic wrap and refrigerate until serving time.

Preheat the oven to 400°F.

Heat the remaining 2 tablespoons oil in a large ovenproof skillet over medium-high heat until it's shimmering but not smoking. Sear the beef so it's browned on all sides, about 10 minutes total. Add the 2 sprigs of rosemary to the skillet and roast the beef in the oven for 15 minutes, or until a thermometer inserted into the thickest part of the meat reaches 125°F. Remove the roast to a cutting board and let rest for 20 minutes. Snip off the kitchen twine and slice the roast into thin slices. Serve the beef on a platter and pass the horseradish sauce around the table.

COOKING TIP

If you really want to take it easy, you can have your butcher tie the tenderloin up for you. It's all easy riding from there.

OVEN-ROASTED RIBS

Serves 4 to 6

Prep time: 15 minutes
Cook time: 1 hour 25 minutes

More often then not, I'll take advantage of our ten months of summer down here and cook my ribs out on the grill. But if you're stuck in one of the forty-seven states that actually experiences winter, oven-roasted ribs are a great option. The best part about ribs is that you can change up the rub and the sauce, giving it more or less heat, depending on your tolerance. Every region in the U.S. lays claim to certain varieties of BBQ sauce. North Carolina favors vinegar, Texas likes tomatoes, and in Kansas City, the sweeter and thicker, the better. I don't really have a dog in this fight; I like what tastes good and I've found that it's hard to beat this simple sauce, which brings together the best of every region's BBQ.

2 tablespoons light brown sugar

1 tablespoon dry mustard

1 tablespoon paprika

2 teaspoons smoked paprika

1 teaspoon freshly ground black pepper

1 teaspoon garlic salt

2 racks baby back pork ribs (4 pounds total)

JAMIE'S TANGY BBQ SAUCE
(MAKES ABOUT 4 CUPS)

1 tablespoon canola oil

$1/2$ small red onion, finely chopped

kosher salt and freshly ground black pepper

$1^1/2$ cups ketchup

1 cup apple cider vinegar

$3/4$ cup light brown sugar

3 tablespoons Dijon mustard

1 tablespoon Worcestershire sauce

2 teaspoons chili powder

$1/2$ teaspoon cayenne pepper

Preheat the oven to 350°F. Line a sheet tray with heavy-duty aluminum foil.

In a small bowl, mix together the brown sugar, mustard, paprika, smoked paprika, black pepper, and garlic salt. Be sure to break up any lumps with your fingers. Reserve 1 tablespoon of rub in a cup for serving.

Remove the silver skin from the underside of the ribs by sliding your fingers under the thin membrane and pulling it off. Repeat this step with the second rack. Rub the ribs with the seasoning mix on both sides. Place the ribs in a single layer on the prepared sheet tray and cover tightly with heavy-duty foil. Bake until the ribs are tender, about 1 hour 15 minutes. (Be careful when removing the foil—there will be hot steam!)

Meanwhile, make the Tangy BBQ Sauce: Heat the oil in a medium saucepan over medium-high heat. Add the onion and cook, stirring, until softened, about 5 minutes. Season with salt and pepper then stir in the ketchup, vinegar, brown sugar, Dijon, Worcestershire sauce, chili powder, and cayenne pepper. Season again with some more salt and black pepper. Bring the sauce to a boil, then reduce to a simmer, set on medium-low heat, and cook until the sauce is thickened, about 35 minutes.

Set your broiler to medium heat. Adjust the shelf so your ribs will be about 5 inches from the heat source.

Broil one rack of ribs at a time until they are nice and brown, about 3 minutes. Remove them from the broiler and brush on some sauce, and then broil again until the sauce is caramelized, about 3 minutes. Repeat with the second rack. (Broiling one rack at a time ensures that you can put each one directly under the broiler.)

Let the racks rest for 5 minutes before slicing them into individual ribs. Sprinkle the cut ribs with the reserved dry rub and serve with extra sauce alongside.

HOBO DINNERS

Pretty much every kid thinks about running away from home at one time or another—and thank goodness most of 'em don't get past the front gate. I imagined following the railroad tracks out of town, thinking that they'd lead me to something magical, or at least away from Albany. There's nothing wrong with my hometown—it still holds a real big place in my heart—but back when I was a kid, I felt the same about Albany as I did about my mom—both were a little embarrassing sometimes, but I couldn't deny that I belonged to them. One word out of my mouth and you knew exactly who and where I came from.

Sometimes Bobby and I would get real serious about moving on. We'd each put some ham sandwiches in a handkerchief, tie it around a long broom handle, and sling it over our shoulders like we had seen Bugs Bunny do on the Saturday morning cartoons. We'd only get a couple of blocks down the street before we ate our sandwiches. Out of food, back home we'd come—just in time for supper.

When I gave up on the idea of living life on the lam, I joined the Boy Scouts of America for some adventure. As a Cub Scout, I loved everything about camping—the fire, ghost stories, sleeping under the stars—everything, that is, except for the food. For dinner we'd put hamburger, potatoes, carrots, and onions in a packet of tinfoil and cook it right there in the campfire. Because there was no temperature gauge, you had to kind of guess when you thought it was cooked through. It was a great idea, but the problem was it didn't actually taste good. It just tasted like fire.

I complained to mom about the "hobo dinners" and she agreed that there was room for improvement. She refined the concept by bringing it indoors and adding some herbs—a foreign concept to the Boy Scouts at the time. I never forgot those foil-packet dinners Mom made and how well the flavors married together. I've included three recipes here that use chicken, fish, and hamburger, and paired them with a seasonal vegetable. If they'd served meals like this back then, I might've made Eagle Scout.

FISH WITH SQUASH AND BUTTER BEANS

Serves 4

Prep time: 10 minutes
Cook time: 20 minutes

I decided to try my hand at cooking fish in a foil packet because I didn't want the juices running all over the oven. More than that, I didn't want to get stuck cleaning it up. But I was actually surprised how good the fish tasted when its flavors married together with the vegetables and herbs in the packet, which you could change out seasonally and get a different dish each time. And the after-dinner cleanup was a snap; I literally tossed out the baking pan.

1 medium zucchini, diced

1 can (15 ounces) butter beans, rinsed and drained

1 cup grape tomatoes, sliced in half

3 cloves garlic, finely chopped

3 tablespoons olive oil

$^1/_4$ cup torn fresh basil leaves

kosher salt and freshly ground black pepper

4 skinless red snapper filets (6 ounces each)

Preheat the oven to 400°F.

In a medium bowl, combine the zucchini, butter beans, tomatoes, garlic, oil, and basil. Season with salt and pepper and toss it all together. Divide the vegetables evenly among four squares of parchment paper placed on four squares of heavy-duty foil. Season the fish on both sides with salt and pepper and place one filet on each square of foil. Make foil pouches by sealing all sides of the foil. Place the sealed packets on a sheet tray and roast for 25 minutes, until the fish is cooked through and the vegetables are soft.

CHICKEN WITH LEEKS AND RUTABAGAS

Serves 4

Prep time: 10 minutes
Cook time: 45 minutes

I always have a lot to say about rutabagas because they're one of my favorite vegetables. They rarely get the praise they deserve, and often get confused with a turnip. Leeks are similar in that some people aren't sure what to do with 'em. Are they scallions? Green onions? They're actually neither. Leeks are a not-too-distant cousin to green onions and garlic, but at the end of the day, the sweet and mild taste of a leek puts it in a category all its own.

3 medium rutabagas, cut into 1/4-inch-thick slices

2 medium leeks, rinsed, trimmed, and sliced

2 teaspoons chopped fresh thyme

1 tablespoon chopped fresh rosemary

3 tablespoons olive oil

kosher salt and freshly ground black pepper

4 boneless chicken breasts (6 ounces each)

2 tablespoons butter, sliced into 1/2 tablespoon pats

Preheat the oven to 350°F.

In a large bowl, combine the rutabagas, leeks, thyme, rosemary, and oil. Season with salt and pepper and toss it all together. Divide and layer the vegetables evenly among four squares of parchment paper placed on four squares of heavy-duty foil. Season the chicken breasts on both sides with salt and pepper and top each vegetable pile with a breast. Spoon any remaining herbs and leeks from the bowl on top of the chicken—you don't want to waste any flavor here. Top each breast with a pat of butter. Make foil pouches by sealing all sides of the foil. Place on a sheet tray and roast for 45 minutes, until the chicken is cooked through and the vegetables are soft.

HAMBURGER WITH CARROTS, POTATOES, AND ONION

Serves 4

Prep time: 10 minutes
Cook time: 40 minutes

This is, quite literally, a meat-and-potatoes kind of recipe, one that I've finessed from my Cub Scout days. If you're looking to make something quick and hearty, this is the meal for you—and nearly every other hungry man on the planet.

1 1/2 pounds ground beef

1/4 cup breadcrumbs

1/2 cup finely grated Parmesan cheese

1 large egg, beaten

1 tablespoon Worcestershire sauce

3 cloves garlic, finely chopped

kosher salt and freshly ground black pepper

1 medium Vidalia onion (or other sweet onion), thinly sliced

2 medium carrots, scrubbed well and sliced 1/4 inch thick

4 medium Yukon gold potatoes, scrubbed well and sliced 1/4 inch thick

2 tablespoons olive oil

Preheat the oven to 350°F. In a large bowl, mix together the beef, breadcrumbs, 1/4 cup Parmesan, egg, Worcestershire, and garlic and season with a good pinch of salt and pepper. Form into four 6-inch patties.

Add the carrots and potatoes to the same bowl, drizzle with the oil and season with salt and pepper. Divide the vegetables evenly among four squares of parchment paper placed on four squares of heavy-duty foil. Top each with a hamburger patty and sprinkle the remaining 1/4 cup Parmesan on top. Make foil pouches by sealing all sides of the foil. Place on a sheet tray and roast for 40 minutes, until the burger is cooked through and the vegetables are soft.

BY SEA

By Sea

Fish can be a hard sell to kids. They're slippery, sometimes smell funny, and you can catch 'em off the end of a dock with a squiggly worm. Part of the problem is that there's little distance between the creature on the end of the hook and the filet on the plate. We call meat from a pig "pork," whereas fish is, well, just fish. In this case, a rose by any other name would mean that a lot more kids would be willing to eat fish.

It took me a long time to come around to eating fish and it wasn't from a lack of exposure. Lake Chehaw is a big beautiful lake, about ten miles wide, in the middle of Albany where Mom and Dad used to take us to catch freshwater fish for dinner. Other times we'd visit my Aunt Glynnis and Uncle Bernie's place in Statesboro, Georgia, which had this quiet pond where we'd fish and swat mosquitoes during long summer evenings. We'd have fish frys with catfish, brim, and crappie, but I never really liked it. Eventually, Bobby and I got smart and we'd catch the fish and release them real quick before Mom and Dad would know what had happened, guaranteeing us hot dogs for dinner.

My palate started to expand when we moved out here to the coast. I've tried more seafood than you can imagine and really started to enjoy certain kinds of fish. I discovered cuts of fish that are similar to steak in texture, like a satisfying salmon "steak," but without any of the heaviness of red meat. And I learned the hard way that quality and freshness matter, but at least I've lived to tell about it.

Today I like fish, especially a flaky white halibut or flounder, just as much as I like steak—but like all meats, preparation is key. With fish, simple, fresh flavors are best—a squeeze of lemon here, a dollop of pesto there. It's good for you, it's easy to prepare, and it cooks quickly. But you don't want to overcook fish because it'll dry out something awful.

What about shrimp, you ask? Shrimp is and always has been my seafood exception. As far as I'm concerned, shrimp doesn't come from the sea, it comes down from Heaven, descending on a buttery cloud of grits.

GRILLED SALMON ON WHITE WINE–SOAKED CEDAR PLANKS

Serves 4

Prep time: 5 minutes
Cook time: 25 minutes

After tearing apart half the North Atlantic fish population trying to find the perfect way to grill fish, I discovered cooking with cedar planks, which sounds more complicated than it is. I just soak the planks in any white wine that I have on hand and source my seasonings from about twenty feet away, plucking lemons from my tree in the backyard and cutting a few sprigs of rosemary from a nearby bush. Fresh homegrown seasonings and a wine-soaked cedar plank? Sounds like a 28 dollar dinner to me.

2 (12 by 6-inch) cedar planks
1 bottle dry white wine
2 skinless salmon filets (1 pound each)
kosher salt and freshly ground black pepper
extra-virgin olive oil
8 lemon slices
6 sprigs fresh rosemary

Soak the cedar planks in white wine in a large baking pan for 2 hours.

Heat your grill on high heat for 15 minutes with the lid closed. Once it's preheated, place the cedar planks directly on the hot grill rack and cook for 1 minute on each side.

Prepare for indirect grilling: Turn off the burner on one side of the grill, and adjust the heat on the other side of the grill to medium-high. Season the salmon on both sides with salt and pepper, then place both filets, skin side down, on the planks. Drizzle the salmon lightly with olive oil and top with the lemon and rosemary. Move the cedar planks to the side of the grill with no heat. Close the lid and cook for 20 to 25 minutes, with the lid closed, until the salmon is opaque and cooked through.

COOKING TIP

The typical cedar planks you see for sale fit a one-pound piece of fish nicely. So for a good-looking presentation, I use two planks.

It's important to soak the planks because otherwise they'll on catch fire. It's wood, y'all.

ROASTED PESTO SALMON WITH GRAPE TOMATOES

Serves 4

Prep time: 5 minutes
Cooking time: 30 minutes

Bobby is a huge fish eater and Brooke likes salmon a lot. I wasn't the biggest fan of creatures of the finned variety, but this recipe changed my tune. I dressed up salmon filets with two things I really love—roasted tomatoes and pesto. It's just as easy as covering the salmon in butter and lemon, but it tastes like you really killed yourself in the kitchen. If you only "kind of" like salmon, try this dish and you'll *really* like salmon—it worked for me.

2 containers (10 ounces each) grape tomatoes

1 tablespoon olive oil

kosher salt and freshly ground black pepper

4 skinless salmon filets (6 ounces each)

1/2 cup Basil Pesto (recipe below)

crushed red pepper flakes (optional)

BASIL PESTO
(MAKES 1 CUP)

4 ounces fresh basil leaves (4 loosely packed cups)

1/2 cup extra-virgin olive oil

1/3 cup finely grated Parmesan cheese

1/4 cup toasted and cooled pine nuts

2 large cloves garlic, peeled

kosher salt and freshly ground black pepper

Preheat the oven to 400°F. Line a sheet tray with foil.

Arrange the tomatoes on the sheet tray, drizzle with olive oil, and season well with salt and pepper. Roast in the oven for 10 minutes.

Meanwhile, make your basil pesto: Add the basil, oil, Parmesan, pine nuts, and garlic to the bowl of a food processor and pulse until the mixture is smooth. Taste for seasoning, adding some salt and pepper.

Season both sides of the salmon filets with salt and pepper. Top each filet with a generous 2-tablespoon dollop of fresh pesto and spread it across the top. (Reserve the remaining 1/2 cup for another use.)

Remove the tomatoes from the oven and add the salmon to the sheet tray. Roast for 10 minutes more, until the tomatoes are soft and the salmon is cooked through. Give the tomatoes one more pinch of salt.

Serve the salmon topped with the roasted tomatoes. Adults can sprinkle the tomatoes with a hit of crushed red pepper flakes for some kick, if they like.

COOKING TIP

Serve this with a side of rice or couscous for an easy weeknight meal. I make my homemade pesto by blending Parmesan, pine nuts, and the basil we get from our herb garden in the summer. The sauce can last up to six months in the freezer, which means you can enjoy this otherwise seasonal dish year-round.

OVEN-ROASTED GARLICKY SHRIMP

Serves 4

Prep time: 5 minutes
Cook time: 10 minutes

Living in Savannah, there's so much shrimp to be had that we've found a million different ways to prepare it. This is a good way that's really simple and you can do it with any type of shrimp found across America. It's no fuss—you just pop it in the oven. If only getting the kids to bed were this easy . . .

1½ pounds large shrimp, peeled and deveined

3 tablespoons olive oil

2 cloves garlic, roughly chopped

1 teaspoon roughly chopped fresh rosemary

kosher salt and freshly ground black pepper

Preheat the oven to 400°F.

On a sheet tray, toss together the shrimp, oil, garlic, and rosemary and season with salt and pepper. Roast for 10 minutes, just until the shrimp is opaque and cooked through (they can get chewy quick).

Transfer the shrimp to a bowl, then pour any remaining garlic and oil from the sheet pan over the shrimp. Y'all can eat as is or serve over rice or a big salad for dinner.

What's ratatouille? Pretty much, it's just a fun way to describe sautéed vegetables. Some chefs can get kind of particular about what defines the traditional dish, but without overthinking it, it's basically a vegetable hash that includes tomatoes, bell peppers, eggplant, zucchini, and basil. The addition of a mild and affordable fish such as halibut upgrades ratatouille from a side dish to a main one.

PAN-ROASTED HALIBUT WITH RATATOUILLE

Serves 4

Prep time: 25 minutes
Cook time: 45 minutes

To make the ratatouille, preheat the oven to 400°F.

Place your tomatoes on a sheet tray, drizzle with 1 tablespoon oil, and season with salt and pepper. Toss it all together and roast for 15 minutes.

To make the ratatouille, heat the remaining 3 tablespoons oil in a large Dutch oven over medium-high heat. Once it's hot, add the onion, garlic, and bell pepper and sauté until they're tender, about 5 minutes. Season with a big hit of salt and pepper. Stir in the tomato paste and cook for 1 minute, continually stirring, toasting it to really develop the flavor. Add the eggplant and zucchini next, and sauté until the eggplant is completely tender, about 6 minutes more. Add the roasted tomatoes and their juices and the stock and simmer until everything is all nice and stew-like, 25 to 30 minutes more. Taste again for seasoning and adjust the salt and pepper as needed. Stir in the basil, butter, and red pepper flakes (or skip the flakes if it's too much heat for your kids). Cover to keep warm.

Meanwhile, in a large nonstick skillet, heat the oil until it shimmers. Pat the fish dry with paper towels and season it on both sides with salt and pepper. Add the halibut to the hot oil and cook over medium heat until nicely browned on the bottom, about 5 minutes. Flip the fish to the other side and cook for about 3 minutes longer.

Garnish with some fresh basil and serve the ratatouille on the side.

RATATOUILLE

2 pints cherry tomatoes

$1/4$ cup olive oil

kosher salt and freshly ground black pepper

1 medium red onion, finely chopped

4 cloves garlic, roughly chopped

1 red bell pepper, chopped

1 tablespoon tomato paste

1 medium eggplant ($1^{1}/_{2}$ pounds), peeled and cut into 1-inch cubes

1 medium zucchini, chopped

1 cup Homemade Chicken Stock (page 205)

$1/4$ cup fresh basil leaves, torn

2 tablespoons butter

$1/8$ teaspoon crushed red pepper flakes (optional)

2 tablespoons olive oil

4 pieces skinless halibut (6 ounces each)

kosher salt and freshly ground black pepper

fresh basil leaves for serving

FROGMORE STEW

Serves 4, generously

Prep time: 10 minutes
Cook time: 40 minutes

A Lowcountry Boil is reason alone for Southerners to gather and celebrate. Its less familiar cousin, Frogmore Stew, is in the same family but carries the traditional name. Frogmore was actually a small fishing community located just outside of Beaufort, South Carolina—a short day trip from Savannah. While the town no longer exists, the legend of where the historic recipe originated endures. It's a very communal meal. All of the ingredients go into one big pot and when it's done cooking, you can just dump it out on some newspaper and stand around the table and eat it. It's not fancy, but there's nothing like it.

2 tablespoons olive oil

1 pound smoked cooked sausage (such as andouille or kielbasa), cut on the bias into 1-inch pieces

1 medium Vidalia onion (or other sweet onion), chopped

2 stalks celery with leaves, chopped

kosher salt and freshly ground black pepper

1/4 cup seafood seasoning (such as Old Bay), plus more for serving

1 bottle (12 ounces) beer

1 tablespoon light brown sugar

2 1/2 quarts water

1 bay leaf

1 head garlic, sliced in half

1 lemon, quartered

3 tablespoons butter

1 pound small new red potatoes

3 ears of corn, husked and cut crosswise into 3 or 4 pieces

4 live blue crabs

1 1/2 pounds large shrimp, shell on

warm bread for serving

hot sauce for serving

Heat the oil in a large stockpot over medium-high heat. Once it's hot, add the sausages and cook, while stirring, until they're nice and browned on all sides, 4 to 5 minutes. Transfer the sausages to a bowl and set aside.

Add the onion and celery to the stockpot and sauté until soft, about 5 minutes. Season the mixture with a big pinch of salt and pepper, then sprinkle in the seafood seasoning and toast, while stirring, for 1 minute. Pour in the beer and scrape up any browned bits that may have stuck to the bottom of the pot. Cook the beer down for 5 minutes; it should reduce by half. Stir in the brown sugar.

Add the water, bay leaf, garlic, lemon, butter, potatoes, and corn. Bring the water up to a simmer, and cook the potatoes halfway through, about 10 minutes. (Insert a paring knife into a potato, there should still be resistance there.)

Add the crabs to the pot, bring the mixture back up to a boil, cover with a lid, and cook for 7 minutes. Add the shrimp and reserved sausage, bring the stew back up to a simmer, and cook for another 5 minutes.

Pour the stew out on a newspaper-lined table. Serve with warm bread, your favorite hot sauce, some Old Bay, and lots of beer.

INGREDIENT NOTE

If you can't find blue crabs in your area, use 2 cups less cooking liquid and omit the step where you add the crabs. Continue to cook the potatoes and corn for 17 minutes before adding the shrimp and sausage. Or feel free to add what you have on hand, like crayfish, instead.

I've never seen picky eaters turn their noses up at Frogmore Stew; there's something in it for everybody.

Shrimp 'n' grits was traditionally a poor man's breakfast for shrimpers in the South Carolina Lowcountry. Today, the dish has gotten a high-class makeover and can be found on five-star menus all over the country. But to me, the best shrimp 'n' grits are still cooked up in the Southeastern kitchens where they originated. I make mine with fresh wild Georgia shrimp that tastes like it was pulled from the net minutes before I brought it home. I've prepared shrimp 'n' grits with barbecue shrimp and a brown sauce, but here we're doing a rich cream sauce that really speaks to our area. It's one of my favorite lunches to cook for Brooke—when we have time to indulge.

CLASSIC SAVANNAH SHRIMP 'N' GRITS

Serves 4

Prep time: 15 minutes
Cook time: 25 minutes

Add the water to a heavy-bottomed saucepan over medium-high heat and season it with salt and pepper. Bring to a simmer, reduce the heat to medium, and pour in the grits in a slow, steady stream while whisking. Cook the grits, stirring occasionally, for about 30 minutes, until they're thick and creamy. Stir in the heavy cream, Parmesan, and butter. Taste your grits for seasoning and adjust as necessary. Cover to keep warm.

Season the shrimp with salt and pepper. Heat the butter and oil in a large sauté pan over medium-high heat until melted and foamy. Add the sausage and onion; sauté until the onion is tender and the sausage is browned, 5 to 6 minutes. Add the shrimp and cook for just 1 minute on each side. Once the shrimp are opaque, remove them with a slotted spoon to a plate and reserve. Add the tomatoes to the pan along with a big pinch of salt and pepper, and cook, stirring, until they have softened and broken down, another 3 to 4 minutes. Stir in the wine and reduce until the mixture is almost dry, about 3 minutes. Stir in the heavy cream and reduce until the sauce can coat the back of a spoon, about 5 minutes more. Return the shrimp to the pan and cook for another minute.

Divide the grits among four bowls and top with a heap of shrimp and sauce. Garnish with some green onions and serve with hot sauce—or don't, if you can't take the heat.

COOKING TIP

Cook quick grits like regular grits—low and slow—so they come out extra creamy.

GRITS

4 cups water

kosher salt and freshly ground black pepper

1 cup quick-cooking grits

1/2 cup heavy cream

2 tablespoons freshly grated Parmesan cheese

2 tablespoons butter

SHRIMP

1 pound large shrimp, peeled and deveined

kosher salt and freshly ground black pepper

1 tablespoon butter

1 tablespoon olive oil

6 ounces finely chopped andouille sausage

1/2 Vidalia onion (or other sweet onion), finely diced

1 small green bell pepper, finely diced

2 medium plum tomatoes, seeded and diced

1/2 cup dry white wine

1/2 cup heavy cream

sliced green onions for serving

hot sauce (optional)

It used to be that only poor folks ate shrimp 'n' grits. Now this dish can run you 28 dollars in New York City at lunchtime.

DRY-BOILED LEMON SHRIMP

Serves 6

Prep time: 10 minutes
Cook time: 15 minutes

Donna Foltz, one of Momma's good friends, hosts a Christmas party every year and asks her guests to bring a dish. And every year, sometime in June, she reminds me to bring my potato salad, which is her favorite. But it's her Dry-Boiled Lemon Shrimp that everyone scrambles to get. I hadn't heard of "dry-boiling" until she showed me the technique; she cooks her shrimp in just a little bit of liquid with a whole lot of seafood and Cajun seasoning.

2 pounds large shrimp, shell on

2 tablespoons seafood seasoning (preferably Zatarain's crab-boil in a bag)

$^1/_2$ teaspoon Cajun seasoning

1 teaspoon kosher salt

1 tablespoon apple cider vinegar

1 small onion, roughly chopped

1 stalk celery, roughly chopped

1 bay leaf

4 sprigs fresh thyme

2 cloves garlic, smashed

4 tablespoons butter, sliced into pats

1 lemon, halved

In a large, heavy-bottomed pot, combine the shrimp, seafood and Cajun seasonings, salt, apple cider vinegar, onion, celery, bay leaf, thyme, and garlic cloves. Top with the butter slices, squeeze in the lemon juice, and toss the lemon peels right into the pot as well. Cover with a lid, turn the heat to medium, and cook for 12 minutes, removing the lid and stirring every few minutes. Turn off the heat and let the shrimp rest for just 3 minutes before serving.

OVEN-FRIED FLOUNDER FILETS

Serves 4

Prep time: 10 minutes
Cook time: 20 minutes

Jack's and Matthew's love of fish is one reason we don't fry in our house. Here, "oven-fried" is code for "baked." Without all that fat and oil, I create that same crunchiness by dredging the filets in panko. The result is a lighter coating that maintains its crispy texture when baked—and I don't have to feel bad when they ask for another "fish stick."

4 large flounder filets (6 to 8 ounces each)

kosher salt and freshly ground black pepper

$^3/_4$ cup all-purpose flour

$^1/_2$ cup whole milk

2 egg whites

2 teaspoons Dijon mustard

$1^3/_4$ cups panko breadcrumbs

$^1/_8$ teaspoon cayenne pepper

1 tablespoon finely chopped fresh parsley

3 tablespoons butter, melted

lemons, cut into wedges, for serving

Preheat the oven to 425°F with a rack in the middle. Line a sheet tray with foil and coat it with nonstick cooking spray.

Pat the fish dry with paper towels and season each side with salt and pepper. Place three baking dishes in front of you. Add the flour to the first; the milk, egg whites, and Dijon to the second (whisking well to combine); and the panko, cayenne, parsley, and butter to the third (tossing them all together really well). Dredge each fish filet first through the flour, then the egg mixture, and finally the panko. Arrange the filets on the sheet tray.

Bake for 15 to 17 minutes, until the filets are just lightly golden and flake easily when poked with a fork. To finish, broil for 1 to 2 minutes until golden brown.

OODLES AND OODLES

Oodles and Oodles

Other than spaghetti or mac 'n' cheese, we didn't have a lot of pasta growing up. Thank goodness, otherwise we'd be big as barn doors. I started to eat more pasta when Jack moved to table food because he liked it so much, but I didn't want a carb overload. Instead, I incorporated as many vegetables and proteins as I could into each dish, playing around with different recipes that would provide a well-balanced meal the whole family could enjoy.

Watching Mario Batali cook has really turned me on to Italian and he's been a huge influence in how I approach pasta. He's such a nice guy and a talented chef who knows his way around linguine better than anyone. In the process, I've gotten smarter about different ways to quickly throw together pasta dishes that are so much more than just noodles and sauce. These days I really enjoy eating pasta, which is good because now that Matthew has come to the table, we're eating pasta more than ever.

I approach pasta as the foundation for a dish. To that I add whatever seasonal vegetables I have on hand, a tasty sauce, and sometimes a protein. Some of my favorite recipes have come about this way, including Autumn Lasagna with Sage and Squash Puree.

Every pasta recipe in this chapter can be modified to meet your needs. Whether you want less vegetables or more protein. The real beauty of these pasta recipes is that you can turn pretty much anything in your fridge—including last night's roasted chicken—into something new and more exciting than leftovers. It's a quick choose-your-own-adventure way of eating that keeps dinnertime interesting—and your refrigerator from overflowing.

THREE-CHEESE STUFFED SHELLS WITH SPINACH AND ZESTY TURKEY TOMATO SAUCE

Serves 10 (5 servings per baking dish)

Prep time: 30 minutes
Cook time: 1 hour

It goes without saying that with kids in the family, we're gonna eat a lot of pasta and cheese. But there is a limit to how much mac 'n' cheese a man can eat—even a Southern one. In this recipe I take what the boys like and present it in something other than the shape of an elbow. Jack loves helping me stuff the shells. The only problem is teaching Matthew that not all shells are fit for eating when we hit the beach.

1 box (12 ounces) jumbo pasta shells

1 tablespoon olive oil

1 pound sweet Italian turkey sausage, casings removed

1 small onion, finely chopped

kosher salt and freshly ground black pepper

2 cloves garlic, finely chopped

1/4 teaspoon crushed red pepper flakes

1 can (28 ounces) crushed tomatoes

1 can (15 ounces) tomato puree

3/4 teaspoon Italian seasoning

1 container (15 ounces) part-skim ricotta cheese

1 package (10 ounces) frozen spinach, defrosted and squeezed of excess water

1/4 cup finely grated Parmesan cheese

2 large eggs, lightly beaten

2 cups shredded part-skim mozzarella cheese

Bring a large pot of salted water to a boil. Cook the shells for 1 minute less than it says on the box. Drain and let cool.

Preheat the oven to 350°F. Spray two 9 by 13-inch baking dishes with nonstick cooking spray.

Heat a large, high-sided skillet over medium-high heat. Add the oil and, once it's hot, add the sausage and cook until browned, stirring and breaking it up with the back of a wooden spoon, for 3 to 4 minutes. Stir in the onion and cook until softened, about 4 minutes more. Season the mixture with a big pinch of salt and pepper, then stir in the garlic and red pepper flakes and cook for 1 minute, until fragrant. Stir in the crushed tomatoes, tomato puree, Italian seasoning, and 1/2 cup water, and simmer it all on medium-low, uncovered, for 15 minutes. Give it a taste for seasoning and add a big pinch of salt if needed.

Meanwhile, add the ricotta, spinach, Parmesan, eggs, and 1 cup mozzarella to a large bowl, season with salt and pepper, and give it a stir until well combined.

Spread 3 ladlefuls of sauce on the bottom of each prepared baking dish. Stuff each shell with 1 heaping tablespoon of cheese mixture. Place twenty stuffed shells in each dish, then cover with even more sauce. Sprinkle each with 1/2 cup mozzarella cheese. Cover with foil and bake for 35 minutes, removing the foil during the last 5 minutes of baking.

If you want to freeze the second dish, make sure it has cooled completely; cover with plastic wrap, then a layer of foil, and freeze for up to 3 months. Remove the baking dish from the freezer and thaw completely in the refrigerator; bake as directed above.

INGREDIENT NOTE

If you're not a fan of turkey sausage, feel free to sub in sweet Italian pork sausages.

COOKING TIP

This recipe makes a double batch, which is great to do when making almost any baked pasta dish since they freeze and reheat so well.

QUICK LEMON AND BASIL LINGUINE

Serves 4 to 6

Prep time: 5 minutes
Cook time: 20 minutes

This is a very simple recipe that's both comforting and delicious, making it perfect for a weekday dinner.

Forget packets of seasoning and powdery orange cheese—quick and affordable cooking doesn't have to mean compromising taste and quality. This one-pot meal literally takes just minutes to prepare, but the addition of fresh lemon zest and strips of basil make it a home run. Move into the next tax bracket by adding chicken or shrimp.

1 pound linguine
$1/4$ cup extra-virgin olive oil
2 cloves garlic, thinly sliced
$1/4$ cup heavy cream
juice from 1 large lemon (about $1/4$ cup)
kosher salt and freshly ground black pepper
$1/2$ cup freshly grated Parmesan cheese, plus more for serving
2 teaspoons lemon zest
$1/2$ cup thinly sliced fresh basil, plus more for serving

In a large pot of boiling salted water, cook the pasta until al dente. Reserve $1/2$ cup of the pasta water, then drain your pasta in a colander.

Heat the oil in the same pot you cooked your pasta in. Once it's hot, add the garlic and cook, stirring, until the edges just begin to turn golden brown, about 2 minutes. Stir in the cream and lemon juice, and season with a pinch of salt and pepper. Simmer for 2 minutes, then toss in the Parmesan, lemon zest, and, finally, the cooked pasta.

Bring the heat to medium and, with tongs, thoroughly toss the pasta through the sauce while drizzling in the reserved $1/2$ cup pasta water, just to loosen up the sauce a bit. Season with freshly ground black pepper and turn off the heat. Toss the pasta with the basil right before serving. Serve in bowls, sprinkled with some extra cheese and torn basil.

COOKING TIP

I like to pick my battles when it comes to getting my kids to eat. While this recipe calls for linguine, if pasta "tunnels" or "wheels" float your kid's boat, then by all means, change it up.

We don't actually have any vegetarians in our family. Not any that we've accepted, anyway.

Lasagna is a dish that I recommend for those of you who are just starting off in the kitchen. It's relatively easy (or pretty hard to screw up, depending on how you want to look at it). Here, we're going homemade with our own creamy béchamel sauce, which is a fancy French way of saying "white sauce." With the addition of seasonal butternut squash and sage, both fresh from our garden, this makes for a big, warm, comforting dish that's a little unexpected. It's so good, even the staunchest carnivores won't notice it's vegetarian; or if they do, they won't care.

AUTUMN LASAGNA WITH SAGE AND SQUASH PUREE

Serves 8

Prep time: 20 minutes
Cook time: 90 minutes

Preheat the oven to 400°F. Line a sheet tray with foil. Place the squash on the sheet tray and drizzle with the oil. Toss well and season with salt and pepper. Roast until soft, about 30 minutes. Transfer to a food processor with the stock; season with salt and pepper, and blend until smooth.

Grease a 13 by 9-inch lasagna pan with butter. Reduce the oven temperature to 375°F.

Melt 8 tablespoons of the butter in a large saucepan over medium heat. Twist and bruise the sage leaves to release their flavor and cook, stirring and flipping and bruising the leaves with a wooden spoon, until they are crisp but the butter is not yet brown. Using a slotted spoon, transfer the sage leaves to a plate and set aside. Sprinkle the flour in the saucepan and stir over medium heat until pasty, about 2 minutes. Slowly pour the milk into the pan, whisking constantly. Return the sage to the milk, and whisk as the mixture comes to a boil. Reduce to a simmer and cook for 15 minutes, stirring every few minutes to keep the sauce from burning onto the bottom of the pan. Season well with salt, pepper, and a dash of nutmeg.

Ladle a thin layer of the sage cream sauce on the bottom of the buttered pan. Lay four lasagna noodles in the pan, overlapping slightly. Add another ladleful of the sauce to cover the noodles, top with one-fourth of the squash puree, then sprinkle with one-fourth of the mozzarella and Parmesan. Repeat layering two more times, then ladle on the remaining white sauce and dollop the lasagna with the squash puree. Sprinkle with the remaining mozzarella and Parmesan and garnish with a few sage leaves. Add the remaining 2 tablespoons of butter to the top. Cover the lasagna tightly with foil and bake for 40 minutes. Remove the foil and bake for another 20 minutes, until golden and bubbling.

1 butternut squash (3 pounds), peeled, seeded, and cut into 1-inch cubes

2 tablespoons olive oil

kosher salt and freshly ground black pepper

1½ cups low-sodium or Homemade Chicken Stock (page 205)

10 tablespoons butter, cut into 1-tablespoon pats, plus more for greasing

8 fresh sage leaves, plus more for serving

½ cup all-purpose flour

4¾ cups whole milk

dash of freshly grated nutmeg

1 box (9 ounces) no-boil lasagna noodles (I like the Barilla brand)

1½ cups grated part-skim mozzarella cheese

½ cup freshly grated Parmesan cheese

SPAGHETTI WITH TURKEY MEATBALLS

Serves 4 to 6

Prep time: 30 minutes
Cook time: 40 minutes

When I was younger, the first dish I ever made to impress a girl was baked spaghetti. I'm not sure what she tired of first—my obsession with comic books or my carbo-loading—but let's just say my love affair with spaghetti far outlasted our love affair. As they say in the South, "Bless her heart." Because this dish is so easy and kids love it, every family has to have it in their weekly rotation. If you're short on time, you can exchange my basic tomato sauce with a store-bought variety. I cut back on fat by using turkey in the meatballs instead of red meat, and baking rather than frying them. My children haven't noticed these small changes. My belt loops have.

1 large egg, lightly beaten

¼ cup whole milk

½ small onion, finely chopped

2 cloves garlic, minced

½ cup panko breadcrumbs

½ cup finely grated Parmesan cheese, plus more for serving

¼ cup finely chopped fresh flat-leaf parsley

1¼ pounds ground turkey (a mix of light and dark meat)

1 tablespoon olive oil

4 cups Basic Tomato Sauce (page 206)

1 pound spaghetti (or your favorite pasta)

Preheat the oven to 400°F. Lightly oil a sheet tray.

In a large bowl, combine the egg, milk, onion, garlic, breadcrumbs, Parmesan and parsley. Fold in the turkey and gently mix all together. Form into 1½-inch golf ball–size meatballs. Place them on the prepared sheet tray, drizzle lightly with olive oil, and bake for 20 to 25 minutes, or until the meatballs are lightly golden and cooked through.

Put the tomato sauce in a large, high-sided skillet or saucepan and bring to a simmer. Add the meatballs and simmer for 10 minutes.

Cook your favorite pasta according to the package directions. Add your pasta to the saucepan with the tomato sauce and meatballs and gently toss it all together.

Serve the spaghetti and meatballs in bowls with some extra Parmesan sprinkled on top.

INGREDIENT NOTE

I like to buy a mixture of white and dark ground turkey (it'll say it right on the label). The dark meat is where you're going to get a lot of the flavor.

COOKING TIPS

Making your own meatballs is super easy—just be sure you have a cover for your pan or it's gonna look like your toddler finger-painted the kitchen with tomato sauce.

Meatballs are a great dish to double up on. Allow the extra meatballs to cool completely after baking, then place them in a single layer on a sheet tray and pop them into the freezer. Once frozen, put 'em in a gallon-size freezer bag, and freeze for up to 3 months. Thaw in the fridge and reheat in a pot of simmering sauce.

CAULIFLOWER MAC 'N' CHEESE

Serves 8

Prep Time: 10 minutes
Cook Time: 45 minutes

Get ready to work some magic. While sneaking cauliflower into traditional mac 'n' cheese doesn't exactly make it low-fat—we're still using whole milk and cheese—it's a great way to cut back on calorie-heavy pasta and throw in some added nutrition. How does it work? The cauliflower absorbs the creamy sauce, disguising the fact that half of this dish is actually vegetable and not macaroni. And if you really don't want to show your hand to your friends and family, keep the recipe's name on the down-low.

8 ounces medium shell pasta (2½ cups)

1 medium head cauliflower (1¾ pounds), cored, cut into small florets then roughly chopped

2 tablespoons butter

½ small onion, finely chopped

2 cloves garlic, chopped

kosher salt and freshly ground black pepper

2 tablespoons all-purpose flour

2½ cups whole milk

2½ cups grated extra-sharp cheddar cheese (10 ounces)

⅓ cup sour cream

1 teaspoon Dijon mustard

1 teaspoon hot sauce

⅛ teaspoon cayenne pepper

1 cup panko breadcrumbs

Preheat the oven to 350°F. Spray a 13 by 9-inch baking dish with nonstick cooking spray.

Bring a large pot of salted water to a boil. Add the pasta and set your timer for 4 minutes less than the time indicated on the back of the package. Add the cauliflower once the timer sounds and cook for 4 minutes more. Be sure the cauliflower is soft and the pasta is cooked through before draining.

Melt the butter in a large saucepan over medium-high heat. Once it's foamy and melted, add the onion and garlic and cook until the onions are softened, about 3 minutes. Season with salt and pepper, then sprinkle in the flour and cook, while stirring, for 1 minute more. Slowly whisk in the milk and bring it to a simmer; the sauce should begin to thicken at this point. Simmer, while stirring, for 5 minutes, until the sauce is thick enough to coat the back of a spoon. Then knock the heat down to low and stir in 2 cups of the cheddar, one handful at a time. Turn off the heat, stir in the sour cream, Dijon, hot sauce, and cayenne, and season the sauce to taste with salt and pepper. Stir in the pasta and cauliflower, making sure both are nice and coated with the sauce.

Pour the pasta and cauliflower mixture into the prepared baking dish. Sprinkle the top with the panko and the remaining ½ cup cheddar.

Bake for 35 minutes, until the top is golden brown and bubbling. Let the mac cool and settle for 5 minutes before digging in.

INGREDIENT NOTE

If you want to lighten this up even more, use reduced-fat (2%) milk instead of whole, part-skim mozzarella in place of the cheddar, and substitute reduced-fat sour cream for the full-fat version.

BACON WRAPPED SHRIMP WITH BASIL PENNE PASTA

Serves 4 to 6

Prep time: 20 minutes
Cook time: 20 minutes

How do you turn something good into something awesome? Wrap it in bacon. This dish will blow you away because you begin with something that's hard to improve upon—plump, colossal shrimp, which really work better than jumbo in this recipe because their size stands up to the strong bacon taste. The trick to this recipe is to bake the bacon halfway before wrapping it around the shrimp, creating a crisp coating for the tender bite tucked inside. The bright freshness of the basil penne pasta pairs perfectly with the rich and savory flavor of the bacon-shrimp bites.

Preheat the oven to 400°F. Line your sheet tray with foil.

Arrange the bacon on the sheet tray and bake until it's halfway done and not yet crisp, about 10 minutes. Remove the bacon to a paper towel–lined sheet tray to drain and cool completely. Drain off and discard all but 1 tablespoon of fat in the pan (you can eyeball this). Once the bacon is cool, wrap each shrimp with a half slice of bacon and line them up, seam side down, on the greased sheet tray. Bake for 10 minutes, until the bacon is crisp and the shrimp are opaque and cooked through.

Add the pasta to a large pot of salted boiling water and cook for the time indicated on the back of the box. Reserve $1/4$ cup of the liquid used to cook the pasta.

Heat the oil in a large skillet over medium-high heat. Add the garlic and tomatoes, give them a stir, and cook until the tomatoes start to soften and melt down, 4 to 5 minutes. Season the tomatoes with a big pinch of salt and pepper. Add the wine and cook, while stirring, until the sauce has begun to thicken, 3 to 4 minutes more. Add the drained pasta to the skillet, along with the reserved pasta cooking liquid, and toss everything together. Adjust your seasoning by adding a little more salt and pepper. Toss in the basil and gently fold in the bacon-wrapped shrimp.

Divide the pasta equally among serving bowls and sprinkle with some Parmesan and red pepper flakes, if desired.

8 bacon slices, cut in half crosswise

1 pound colossal shrimp (13 to 15 per pound), peeled and deveined

1 pound penne pasta

$1/4$ cup olive oil

4 cloves garlic, roughly chopped

1 pound grape tomatoes, sliced in half

kosher salt and freshly ground black pepper

$1/2$ cup dry white wine

$1/4$ cup fresh basil leaves, torn

Parmesan cheese for serving (optional)

crushed red pepper flakes for serving (optional)

BAKED EGGPLANT RIGATONI WITH FOUR CHEESES

Serves 8

Prep time: 20 minutes
Cook time: 1 hour 10 minutes

Beware of the sponge-like potential of eggplant. If you fry it as opposed to baking it, the eggplant soaks up every bit of oil you add, so you'll just keep adding more and more and more . . .

It took me some time to get up the nerve to cook with eggplant because I just couldn't wrap my head around the notion that it's a passable substitute for meat in any recipe. However, it does in fact add a satisfying meaty quality without all the excess oil and fat. I'm not about to become a full-fledged vegetarian over it, but I can testify that this eggplant and noodle dish is a tasty option.

1 small eggplant (1¼ pounds), peeled and cut into 1-inch cubes

¼ cup olive oil

kosher salt and freshly ground black pepper

3 cups Basic Tomato Sauce (page 206)

2 tablespoons torn fresh basil

1 pound rigatoni pasta

8 ounces fresh mozzarella, diced

1 cup part-skim ricotta cheese

¾ cup grated Fontina cheese

¼ cup finely grated Parmesan cheese

Preheat the oven to 400°F. Spray a 13 by 9-inch baking dish with nonstick cooking spray.

Place the eggplant on a sheet tray, drizzle with the oil, and season with salt and pepper. Toss well to combine. Roast the eggplant until golden, 30 to 35 minutes.

Transfer the eggplant to a large saucepan, cover with the tomato sauce, and stir in the basil. Bring the whole thing up to a simmer and cook for 5 minutes to blend all the flavors together. Taste for seasoning and adjust accordingly.

Drop the oven temperature down to 350°F.

Cook the pasta in boiling salted water according to package instructions. Drain well, reserving ½ cup pasta cooking liquid from the pot.

Add the pasta to the eggplant sauce and stir to combine, adding ¼ cup pasta cooking liquid to loosen up the sauce, only if needed. Transfer the eggplant pasta to the prepared baking dish. Stir in the mozzarella and dollop with the ricotta, giving it a gentle stir but not mixing the ricotta completely into the sauce. Top the whole thing off with the Fontina and Parmesan. Bake for 35 minutes, until bubbly and golden on top.

PICK A SIDE

Pick a Side

When it comes to side dishes, anything goes. From something as simple as a single dill pickle to the more complex baked Wild Rice and Swiss Chard Gratin, a side dish really rounds out a meal. That's not to say that all sides are created equal. Anyone who's ever been served lasagna with a side of mac 'n' cheese knows what I mean; it's all about successful pairing—choosing the right flavors, textures, and even colors to complement the main dish. As good as a green bean casserole may be, pair it with braised collards and a warm spinach salad and you risk turning green just looking at your plate.

When invited to a dinner party, guests are often asked to bring a side, so it's good to have some go-to recipes in your arsenal. Some people even become known for their well-loved side dishes. My mom, for instance, is always asked to bring her mac 'n' cheese. Brooke brings her popular strawberry pretzel salad that I refer to as Yes, a Jelly Salad (the jury is still out on whether this is a salad or a dessert, see page 172). The recipes in this chapter are some of the sides that have been requested of me time and time again by my family and friends alike. I've also included some tips about which foods these dishes pair well with to help you make a good match (Mexican rice with lasagna, for instance, is not a great combination).

The recipes in this chapter complement just about any main dish, travel well, and pretty much guarantee you'll get an invite back—if you want it. If not, bring a bag of chips. Half-eaten.

SHAVED BRUSSELS SPROUTS WITH BACON AND PECANS

Serves 4 to 6

Prep time: 10 minutes
Cook time: 15 minutes

It's no wonder this dish is so good. You could put bacon and brown sugar on a paper plate and it'd be delicious.

You probably wouldn't ever put a Brussels sprout and a bikini model together, but it happens to be a pretty fantastic pairing. My mom called me one day and said, "I've got a *Sports Illustrated* swimsuit model on the show today; would you like to be on the show, too?" Well, a son's gotta do what a son's gotta do. So I said to my wife, "Momma told me I have to be on her show today." It was really nice to meet this swimsuit model, but honestly, my favorite part of that day was when said model showed me how to make Brussels sprouts so they taste good. Cabbage is one of my favorite vegetables, so I thought that I would love Brussels sprouts because they're pretty much tiny cabbages. But they're *real* bitter. The trick to getting rid of that bitterness—and pretty much the secret to making any great dish—is that you've got to add a little bit of bacon and a little bit of sugar. This recipe here is a winner—a top model, dare I say.

1½ pounds Brussels sprouts, ends trimmed

2 slices thick-cut bacon, sliced into ¼-inch strips

½ medium red onion, finely chopped

½ cup roughly chopped pecans

2 tablespoons apple cider vinegar

1 tablespoon light brown sugar

kosher salt and freshly ground black pepper

Cut the Brussels sprouts in half, put them face down, and thinly slice into ribbons. If this is just too tedious for you, an easier way to prep them is to slice them in a food processor fitted with a thin slicing disk.

Add the bacon to a large skillet over medium heat and slowly render out its fat. Continue cooking until the bacon is nice and crisp, 3 to 4 minutes total. Using a slotted spoon, transfer the bacon to a paper towel–lined plate and set it aside just for the time being.

Turn the heat up to medium-high, add the onion, and sauté until it's softened, about 3 minutes. Stir in the Brussels sprouts and sauté until they're tender-crisp, about 5 minutes. Stir in the pecans and cook, while stirring, for another minute, then stir in the vinegar and brown sugar and season it all to taste with salt and pepper. Cook and stir for 1 minute more, stirring.

Transfer the Brussels sprouts to a bowl and sprinkle the reserved bacon over the top before serving it up.

CAST-IRON SKILLET CREAMED CORN

Serves 4 to 6

Prep time: 20 minutes
Cook time: 15 minutes

Canned creamed corn. Is. Not. Good. But for some reason, it's something people don't think to make at home. It's one of my favorite things that my mom makes and one of the most popular dishes we have at the restaurant. This side is traditionally hearty, usually calling for a cup of heavy cream. But here we lighten it up a bit by using a half cup of cream and a half cup of chicken stock, keeping the smoky, sweet and creamy taste, but cutting out a few of the calories.

6 medium ears of corn, husked
2 slices bacon, sliced into $1/2$-inch pieces
1 shallot, minced
2 teaspoons chopped fresh thyme
kosher salt and freshly ground black pepper
$1/2$ cup heavy cream
$1/2$ cup Homemade Chicken Stock (page 205)
1 tablespoon butter
1 green onion, thinly sliced
2 teaspoons sugar (optional)

Cut the kernels from the corncobs and place in a medium bowl, making sure to use your knife to scrape off all the pulp and milk from the cobs into the bowl.

In a cast-iron skillet set over medium heat, cook the bacon, stirring, until crisp, about 4 minutes. Transfer with a slotted spoon to a paper towel–lined plate and set aside.

Add the shallot to the same pan and sauté until softened, about 2 minutes. Stir in the corn with its pulp and the thyme and season with salt and pepper. Sauté for 2 minutes, until the thyme is fragrant and the corn starts to turn lightly golden. Pour in the cream and stock and simmer for 5 minutes, or until the corn is just tender.

Transfer 1 cup of the corn mixture to a food processor or blender and puree until it's smooth. Then place the pureed corn back into the skillet and fold in the butter, reserved bacon, and green onion. Taste for seasoning, adding sugar if your corn isn't sweet enough, and salt and pepper.

COOKING TIP

Pureeing a cup of the corn kernels adds a smooth texture to the creamed corn.

WILD RICE AND SWISS CHARD GRATIN

Serves 4 to 6

Prep time: 15 minutes (plus time to cook the rice)
Cook time: 50 minutes

What is a "gratin"? It basically refers to any dish with a brown, crusty top that comes from baking or broiling cheese, butter, or breadcrumbs. For many of us, that crusty bit is the most coveted part of the casserole. Like the edge of a brownie or the top of a muffin, it's where the goods are. I get tired of eating the same ol' rice, so here I give the starch staple a kick in the pants, transforming it from a low-brow side to a member of the "upper crust"—a worthy accompaniment to Sunday's roast chicken.

4 tablespoons butter, plus more for greasing

1 cup wild rice blend

1 bunch Swiss chard (1 pound), leaves removed from center ribs and stems

1 medium onion, finely chopped

kosher salt and freshly ground black pepper

3 cloves garlic, finely chopped

2 teaspoons chopped fresh thyme

2 tablespoons all-purpose flour

1¼ cups whole milk

1 tablespoon dry sherry

dash of freshly grated nutmeg

⅓ cup panko breadcrumbs

¼ cup freshly grated Parmesan cheese

1 tablespoon olive oil

INGREDIENT NOTE

Swiss chard, a close relative of the garden beet, is available year-round and has tons of nutrients. It's kind of bitter by itself, but when cooked into this dish, it adds another flavor dimension.

Preheat the oven to 350°F. Grease a 2-quart baking dish with butter.

Cook the rice as directed on the package. Meanwhile, bring a large pot of salted water up to a boil. Trim off the tough bottoms of the Swiss chard stems. Slice the stems and ribs into ½-inch pieces, add to the boiling water, and cook for 2 minutes. Roughly chop the greens, then add them to the boiling water by handfuls; cook for 3 minutes more, until the stems and leaves are tender. Drain the greens in a colander and rinse with cold water to stop the cooking. Once cool, wrap the greens in a clean kitchen towel and gently squeeze out all the liquid. Unwrap and give the greens another chop.

Melt the butter in a large saucepan over medium heat. Add the onion and sauté until softened, about 5 minutes. Season with salt and pepper, then stir in the garlic and thyme, cooking for about 1 minute, or until nice and fragrant. Sprinkle in the flour and cook, while stirring, for about 1 minute more. Pour in the milk, stirring constantly, and bring the mixture up to a simmer. Cook for 5 minutes, or until thick, then season with the sherry, nutmeg, and another pinch of salt and pepper. Turn off the heat and fold in your cooked rice and Swiss chard.

Transfer the wild rice mixture to the prepared baking dish. In a small bowl, mix the breadcrumbs together with the Parmesan and oil. Evenly top the baking dish with the breadcrumb mixture. Bake for 25 to 30 minutes, until bubbly and golden.

Normally, I'd rather eat more meatloaf and less potato. This dish is the one exception.

When I want to do a real special dinner for Brooke, I include this potato gratin, an easy-to-put-together side that tastes super-delicious. It's a once- or twice-a-year kind of dish because it's so heavy and rich. You can blame the cream and cheeses. Or you can thank the cream and cheeses. This goes great with roast beef tenderloin or roast pork loin.

CREAMY POTATO GRATIN

Serves 4 to 6

Prep time: 10 minutes
Cook time: 1 hour 20 minutes

Preheat the oven to 350°F. Grease a 2-quart baking dish with butter.

Add the heavy cream, shallot, garlic, thyme, and just a pinch of salt and pepper to a medium saucepan and bring to a simmer.

Add the potatoes to the saucepan, give them a stir, and cook for 4 minutes, stirring on occasion, until you see the liquid thicken up. Remove and discard the thyme.

Pour half of the potato mixture into the prepared baking dish. Give the dish a shake to help the potato slices settle into an even layer. Sprinkle with salt and pepper and half the cheddar and Parmesan. Pour in the remaining potatoes and cream, then top with the rest of the cheddar and Parmesan, along with one final seasoning of salt and pepper.

Cover tightly with foil, place on a sheet tray, and bake for 1 hour. Remove the foil and continue to bake until golden and bubbly, 10 to 15 minutes more.

INGREDIENT NOTE

For a more grown-up flavor, substitute Gruyère in place of the cheddar and add a dash of nutmeg.

COOKING TIP

Use a mandoline to create thin, even slices of potato. This dish can be made a day ahead and reheated in a 350°F oven.

butter, for greasing

2 cups heavy cream

1 shallot, minced

2 cloves garlic, minced

1 sprig fresh thyme

kosher salt and freshly ground black pepper

1¾ pounds Yukon gold potatoes, well scrubbed and cut crosswise into ⅛-inch-thick slices

1 cup shredded sharp cheddar cheese

¼ cup freshly grated Parmesan cheese

MOMMA'S ROASTED ACORN SQUASH WITH BROWN SUGAR

Serves 4

Prep time: 10 minutes
Cook time: 1 hour

Jack and I started a little garden together at the house and we were pretty certain we planted yellow squash. But instead, acorn squash miraculously appeared. Of course he expected me to do something really fabulous with his prize squash, but I didn't have a clue as to how to prepare it. Luckily Momma came to my rescue and showed me this simple recipe. This dish is both a little bit sweet and a little bit savory: The fresh thyme kicks up the savory element, balancing out the brown sugar and maple syrup. Jack ended up loving this recipe, but I can't help but think that pride for his homegrown squash had a little something to do with it.

2 medium acorn squash

5 tablespoons butter, at room temperature

3 tablespoons light brown sugar

2 tablespoons real maple syrup

2 teaspoons chopped fresh thyme

kosher salt and freshly ground black pepper

Preheat the oven to 400°F. Line a sheet tray with foil.

Slice each squash in half. Use a spoon to scoop out the seeds and discard them. Arrange the squash, cut sides up, on a sheet tray.

Combine the butter, brown sugar, maple syrup, thyme, and salt and pepper in a saucepan and bring to a boil. Remove from the heat and divide the melted butter mixture among the squash cavities, brushing some on the cut side of each squash. Bake for about 1 hour, until the squash is tender when pierced with a fork.

ROASTED CAULIFLOWER WITH CRANBERRIES

Serves 4 to 6

Prep time: 15 minutes
Cook time: 20 minutes

If you've only had cauliflower steamed, there's a good chance you wouldn't go out of your way to make it at home. But there are a few simple steps that help maximize cauliflower's potential as a tasty side dish. Drizzling it with olive oil and roasting it in the oven draws out the flavor. Adding cranberries and almonds gives it sweetness, texture and color. In the end it's really pretty, and more than that, it's delicious.

1 large head cauliflower (about 2 pounds), cored and cut into florets

1/4 cup olive oil

4 cloves garlic, roughly chopped

kosher salt and freshly ground black pepper

1/2 cup dried cranberries

1/2 cup roasted and salted almonds, chopped

2 tablespoons roughly chopped fresh parsley

1 tablespoon lemon juice

Preheat the oven to 450°F.

Place the cauliflower on a sheet tray and drizzle with the oil. Toss in the garlic and sprinkle with a big pinch of salt and pepper. Use your hands to mix it all together. Roast the cauliflower for about 20 minutes, flipping with a spatula halfway through cooking, until it's golden in spots and soft.

Transfer the cauliflower to a large serving bowl. While it's still hot, toss with the cranberries, almonds, parsley, and lemon juice. Taste for seasoning, adding more salt and pepper if you think it needs it.

MOMMA'S MASHED RUTABAGAS

Serves 6

Prep time: 10 minutes
Cook time: 50 minutes

It took me about thirty years to eat a rutabaga and I've been trying to catch up ever since. If you don't like 'em, you haven't had them done properly. My mom substituted them for mashed potatoes one night and I was surprised at their earthy-sweet flavor. They're creamy and delicious; underrated and underused. Farmers have been growing rutabagas—which are said to have evolved from a cabbage and a turnip—for more than 200 years in this country, but they're still a novelty at most American tables. Not mine.

3 medium (baseball-size) rutabagas (1 1/2 pounds), peeled and chopped

2 russet potatoes (1 1/2 pounds), peeled and chopped

1/2 cup whole milk

4 ounces cream cheese, at room temperature, cut into chunks

4 tablespoons butter, sliced into pats

kosher salt and freshly ground black pepper

Add the rutabagas to a large pot of cold salted water. Place over medium-high heat and bring the water up to a boil. Reduce the heat to a simmer and cook for about 30 minutes. Add the potatoes to the pot and cook for 15 to 20 minutes more, until both the potatoes and rutabagas are tender. Drain well. In the same pot over medium heat, combine the milk, cream cheese, and butter, stirring to melt, and seasoning with a big pinch of salt and pepper. Return the potatoes and rutabagas back to the pot and mash them up real well. Have a taste for seasoning and adjust as necessary.

GREEK SALAD COUSCOUS

Serves 6

Prep time: 15 minutes
Cook time: 5 minutes

There's a Greek restaurant we really like here in town and this recipe is like bringing those wonderful flavors home.

My brother started cooking with couscous a long time ago—way before it was ever trendy around here. And we'd make so much fun of him, mainly because we couldn't figure out what he was eating. A grain? Pasta? *Sand?* We weren't too far off. Couscous is actually a coarsely ground pasta made from wheat. And while colors and layers of flavor are important in most dishes, they're super-important in this one because, on its own, couscous doesn't taste like much. In this Greek-influenced dish, we're pulling out all the tricks by incorporating feta, fresh herbs, olives, and cucumbers. The salad holds up really well as a second-day dish.

1 cup couscous

1 small shallot, finely chopped

1 English cucumber, diced

1 1/4 cups grape tomatoes, sliced in half (a mix of red and yellow looks nice)

1/2 cup Kalamata olives, pitted and sliced in half

2 tablespoons chopped pepperoncini peppers

1/2 cup crumbled feta cheese

2 tablespoons chopped fresh parsley

2 tablespoons chopped fresh dill

3 tablespoons olive oil

2 tablespoons red wine vinegar

kosher salt and freshly ground black pepper

Bring 2 cups of lightly salted water to a boil. Stir in the couscous, cover with a lid, and remove from the heat. Set a timer for 5 minutes. When the timer goes off, remove the lid, fluff the couscous with a fork, and transfer to a large mixing bowl. Let the couscous cool completely.

Once cool, add all the remaining ingredients and toss together really well. Taste for seasoning, adjusting with more salt and pepper, as necessary.

INGREDIENT NOTE

Pepperoncini are pickled peppers that pack a tangy bite. They add a little heat to this dish and some crunch.

Matthew is violently allergic to rice. His doctors say he may grow out of his allergy and I hope he does, because when it comes to food, that kid doesn't discriminate.

There are a million different ways to serve rice and one that I particularly like is rice salad. This is a flavorful side dish with a lot of texture and crunch. It holds well so leftovers make the perfect next-day lunch; serve cold on a bed of arugula. The curry in this dish may be an acquired taste for some kids, but familiar ingredients such as raisins, apples, and pistachios—some of Jack's favorite things—will encourage them to give this salad a try.

Heat the oil in a medium saucepan over medium-high heat. Once it's hot, sprinkle the curry powder into the oil, and cook, while stirring, for 30 seconds, until fragrant. Stir in the rice and cook for 1 minute, then add the water and season with salt and pepper. Bring to a boil, reduce to a simmer, cover, and cook until the rice is tender, about 45 minutes. Remove from the heat, sprinkle the raisins over the rice, cover, and let the rice mixture steam for 15 minutes. Fluff with a fork, then transfer to a large bowl to cool.

Add the celery, apple, green onions, and pistachios to the cooled rice. Drizzle with the lime juice, season with salt and pepper, and toss it all together.

INGREDIENT NOTE

Brown rice is a triple threat: It adds nice color, a nutty flavor, and it's more nutritious than white rice.

COOKING TIP

Toasting the curry powder brings out its pungent flavor. I like to use a mild curry powder to keep the heat in check.

CRUNCHY CURRIED RICE SALAD WITH APPLES AND GREEN ONIONS

Serves 6

Prep time: 15 minutes
Cook time: 1 hour

2 tablespoons olive oil

1 tablespoon curry powder

1 cup long-grain brown rice

2 cups water

kosher salt and freshly ground black pepper

1/2 cup raisins

1 stalk celery, chopped

1 apple, washed and thinly sliced

4 green onions, thinly sliced

1/3 cup chopped, roasted and shelled pistachios

juice of 1 lime

AUNT PEGGY'S CUCUMBER SALAD

Serves 6

Prep time: 15 minutes
Cook time: 20 minutes
(plus 20 minutes marinatin')

Aunt Peggy has served this fresh and tangy cold salad at every meal my whole life—every lunch, every dinner, every day. It's a classic recipe—not because my great aunt made it, but because *everybody's* great aunt made it. In my version, I cut down on the onion and added honey to sweeten up the dressing just a bit, making this salad more kid-friendly but every bit as memorable.

2 cucumbers (about 2 pounds), peeled and thinly sliced

1 pint grape tomatoes, sliced in half

1/4 medium Vidalia onion (or other sweet onion), very thinly sliced

2 tablespoons chopped fresh parsley

kosher salt and freshly ground black pepper

2 tablespoons apple cider vinegar

1 tablespoon olive oil

2 teaspoons honey

In a large serving bowl, toss together the cucumbers, tomatoes, onion, and parsley. Sprinkle with a little salt and pepper.

In a small mixing bowl, combine the vinegar, oil, honey, and salt and pepper, whisking until the honey is dissolved. Pour the dressing over your salad and let stand for about 20 minutes before serving to allow the flavors to develop.

BROCCOLI AND BACON TWICE-BAKED POTATOES

Serves 4

Prep time: 20 minutes
Cook time: 1 hour 30 minutes

Unless you just came out of the woods, one of these potatoes could easily be satisfying enough for your whole dinner.

I got my first hundred dollar tip while working at a place called The Oyster Bar when I was in college. A guy and his two sons had just come out of the woods after hunting for three or four days and they were starving. The owner of the place, Chuck, was really big on twice-baked potatoes at the time, putting shrimp or strips of sirloin steak and cheese in them rather than just on top. I discovered that extra step makes all the difference. I piled those potatoes on that man and his sons and they threw down. That hundred dollars disappeared real fast, but the twice-baked-potato technique stuck. This is my version. Tips are always welcome.

4 large russet potatoes (12 ounces each), well scrubbed and dried

1 crown broccoli (10 ounces), cut into florets

2 tablespoons olive oil

6 slices bacon

3 green onions, thinly sliced

1 cup grated sharp cheddar cheese, plus more for serving

3/4 cup sour cream

4 tablespoons butter

kosher salt and freshly ground black pepper

Preheat the oven to 425°F.

Prick the potatoes with a fork. Place them on the top rack of your oven and bake for 1 hour, or until tender. Meanwhile, place the broccoli on a sheet tray, drizzle with the oil and roast for 18 to 20 minutes, until tender-crisp. Lay the bacon on a foil-lined sheet tray. Bake for 10 to 12 minutes, or until crisp. Transfer your bacon to a paper towel–lined plate to drain.

Turn your oven temperature down to 350°F.

Once the bacon, broccoli, and potatoes are cool to the touch, chop the bacon and broccoli and add to a mixing bowl. Slice off the top third of the potatoes and scrape any potato from the tops into the mixing bowl, discarding the skins. Using a spoon, scrape the flesh from the four potatoes into the mixing bowl (but keep the skins!). Add the green onions, cheddar cheese, sour cream, butter, and a big pinch of salt and pepper. Mash the potatoes, mixing everything together really well. Taste for seasoning, adding more salt and pepper if you need it. Put the potato mixture back into their skins. Place them on a sheet tray and sprinkle each potato with a little more cheese. Bake for 20 to 25 minutes, until the filling is hot and the cheese is melted.

BRAISED GREENS

Serves 6 to 8

Prep time: 20 minutes
Cook time: 30 minutes

We're getting back to the basics here. Old-fashioned Southern dishes are trending big time in fancy restaurants across the United States—even jumping the pond in some cases. But if y'all "aren't from around here" and are unsure how to handle these massive, leafy greens, let me be your guide. Braising greens is a quick way to prepare this Southern staple, while still infusing them with the big smoky flavor they're known for.

1 bunch kale (1 pound)

1 bunch mustard greens (1 pound)

1 bunch collard greens (1 pound)

3 strips thick-sliced bacon, chopped

1 medium onion, chopped

3 cloves garlic, chopped

kosher salt and freshly ground black pepper

2 cups Homemade Chicken Stock (page 205)

1 tablespoon apple cider vinegar

1 tablespoon light brown sugar

1/8 teaspoon crushed red pepper flakes

Make sure your sink is nice and clean and then fill it with cold water. Strip the kale leaves from their stems, tear the leaves into pieces, and toss the leaves into the water. Repeat with the mustard greens. To trim the collard greens, strip the leaves off the stems and add these to the sink as well. Agitate the water with your hands, making sure all the greens get cleaned. Remove the collard greens first; pile them up, roll into a cigar, and slice into 1/2-inch strips. Transfer all the greens to a large colander to drain.

Place the bacon in a large Dutch oven and turn the heat to medium. Cook, stirring, until the bacon is crisp and the fat is rendered, 5 to 6 minutes. Transfer the bacon with a slotted spoon to a paper towel–lined plate and set aside.

Add the onion and garlic to the Dutch oven and sauté until soft, about 4 minutes, seasoning really well with salt and pepper. Begin adding the greens in bunches, using tongs to toss them in the pot so they wilt down a bit before adding another batch. Repeat until all the greens are in the pot. Season with another big pinch of salt and pepper then pour in the stock, cider vinegar, brown sugar, and red pepper flakes. Bring the broth to a boil, then reduce the heat to medium, cover with a lid, and braise for about 10 minutes. Remove the lid and cook for about 10 minutes more, tossing on occasion, until the greens are real nice and tender.

QUICK SAUTÉED MIXED VEGGIES AND HERBS

Serves 4

Prep time: 5 minutes
Cook time: 15 minutes

It's time to break out of the canned vegetables routine. When you need a quick and summery side dish, preparing this mix of fresh seasonal vegetables takes just a bit longer than it does to turn the can opener, but it's so worth it. Luckily, both of our boys love vegetables, so Brooke and I make this recipe all the time. Like most gardens, ours gets overrun with zucchini and squash, which come in all at once. This is our favorite way to handle the harvest.

2 tablespoons olive oil

2 medium zucchini, chopped

1 medium yellow squash, chopped

kosher salt and freshly ground black pepper

3 cloves garlic, roughly chopped

$1/3$ cup frozen peas, thawed

2 tablespoons roughly chopped fresh basil

2 tablespoons roughly chopped fresh mint

Heat the oil in a large skillet over medium-high heat. Once it's hot, toss in the zucchini and yellow squash, and sauté until the veggies are softened and lightly browned, 8 to 10 minutes. Season the veggies with a good pinch of salt and pepper. Stir in the garlic and peas and cook for another 2 to 3 minutes, or until the peas are heated through and the garlic is softened and fragrant. Toss in the herbs at the last minute and mix it up well.

COOKING TIP

Transform this into a main course by tossing in some cooked pasta at the last minute. I know you can't find *that* in a can.

THE PAYOFF

The Payoff

Contrary to what some people may think, I didn't grow up finishing off dinner with a piece of Mom's Gooey Butter Cake every night, though that would've been pretty awesome. Dessert was actually something we reserved for special occasions, like birthdays or Christmas dinner. Our family saw sweets as a celebration food—something we really looked forward to and appreciated because it was a novelty at our table.

Because of this, I don't really have much of a sweet tooth, but I do like dessert when we're enjoying a meal with friends. By the end of the meal, everyone is relaxed, the conversation is easy, and our bellies are full—but never too full for a taste of something sweet, like my brightly flavored Best Lemon Tart or the mouthwatering Peach and Blackberry Cobbler. Our kids like the idea of dessert, but rarely do they chow down. Instead, they excitedly enjoy a few bites and then go back to playing while the adults genuinely savor every bite.

While my boys love every dessert in this chapter, it was important to me to develop recipes sophisticated enough for a grown-up palate. Every dessert is baked, and almost all incorporate fruit in some form, a reflection of my personal bias. I prefer the flakiness of a baked dessert and the natural sweetness fresh fruit supplies. I don't gravitate toward overly gooey, greasy desserts, and we have so many wonderful peaches, lemons, and strawberries around here—some grow in my backyard—it would be an oversight not to include them.

Note, when the need arises, I'm not above bribing my kids with dessert to get them to eat their dinner. A tempting sweet treat can serve as the proverbial carrot (cake) dangling on a stick, getting kids—or me—to do just about anything. But in my case, it's one hundred sit-ups.

BAKED APPLE TURNOVERS

Makes 8 pastries

Prep time: 10 minutes
Cook time: 30 minutes

I bet you wouldn't be shocked to know that my mom used to make deep-fried apple pies back when I was Jack's age. She would wrap apples and brown sugar in biscuit dough and drop it into a sizzling vat of oil. I loved those pies so much, but they didn't do much for my health. In our own house, Brooke and I have never deep-fried a thing. Not one time—and we've lived here for eight years. Instead, we do a lot of baking. By baking instead of frying, I can pass along this slightly revised family recipe, sharing the memories and flavors with the people I love but in a healthier way. I use fresh apples for the filling and just a little bit of brown sugar, then fold it up in ready-made puff pastry, which cooks up to be much lighter and flakier than a dense biscuit dough. Jack gets to enjoy the same dessert that I had when I was a fat little boy, except he's not a fat little boy.

2 tablespoons butter

2 Honeycrisp apples, peeled, cored and chopped into 1/2-inch cubes

2 Granny Smith apples, peeled, cored and chopped into 1/2-inch cubes

3/4 cup firmly packed light brown sugar

1 tablespoon all-purpose flour, plus more for dusting

3/4 teaspoon ground cinnamon

1/2 teaspoon ground ginger

1/8 teaspoon kosher salt

1 large egg

1 tablespoon water

1 package (17.3 ounces) puff pastry, thawed

1 tablespoon granulated sugar for sprinkling

COOKING TIPS

The filling can be made up to two days in advance—but I bet you won't be able to wait that long to use it.

Little cooks can help roll out the puff pastry, add the filling, brush with egg wash and sprinkle with sugar.

Melt the butter in a large sauté pan over medium-high heat until it's foamy. Add the apples and cook, while stirring, for 3 minutes, or until they're slightly softened. Stir in the brown sugar, flour, cinnamon, ginger, and salt, and continue cooking, stirring, for 3 minutes more, or until the pan looks almost dry and the sugar is syrupy. Remove the apples to a bowl and cool them completely.

Preheat the oven to 400°F and adjust your oven racks to the center. Line two sheet trays with parchment paper. In a small bowl, whisk together the egg and water and set it aside.

One at a time, very carefully unfold your sheets of puff pastry on a lightly floured work surface. Roll out each sheet to an 11 by 11-inch square. Cut each sheet into four equal-size squares and place them on the prepared sheet trays. Brush the outside corners of each square with some egg wash and add a scant 1/3 cup filling across the center of each square, going from one corner to the other. Fold the top corner over the filling and press it to seal. Then fold the bottom corner over the last fold and press it to seal. (Two corners of the tart will remain open with the filling peeking out.) Repeat this step with the remaining squares of pastry. Brush the outside of each turnover with egg wash and sprinkle lightly with sugar. Bake for 20 minutes, until puffy and golden. Allow the turnovers to cool a bit before serving.

Jack and I eat
these together
and then we sit
back together and
rub our tummies.

To earn money to go to the Albany fair, Momma had Bobby and me sell pecans. She took us around the neighborhood to all the pecan trees and we'd have to collect them into buckets. I always loved that fair, but hated pecans for a real long time. My relationship with pecans has since improved. We have four trees at our house, and when Jack was a bitty baby, I'd carry him around in my arms, pointing things out to him saying, "This is grass. This is a tree. This is a pecan." He got real excited about the pecans. It blew his mind that he could find food outside on the ground. Because pecans are such a big part of our lives and Southern culture in general, I wanted to include a pecan pie recipe. This one riffs on tradition just a bit: A pretzel crust and the palate-pleasing flavor of salted caramel are sure to land this divine dessert on your short list.

SALTED CARAMEL PECAN PIE WITH PRETZEL CRUST

Serves 8

Prep time: 15 minutes
Cook time: 1 hour 5 minutes

Preheat the oven to 350°F.

Add the pretzel crumbs, flour, sugar, and melted butter to a medium bowl and stir until combined. Dump the crumb mixture into a 9-inch deep-dish pie plate and press it evenly around the bottom and sides of the pan. Place the pie plate on a sheet tray to catch drips and bake for 10 minutes, until the crust is firm.

In a medium saucepan over medium heat, combine the brown sugar, corn syrup, butter pieces, and sea salt and bring it up to a boil, while stirring. Remove from the heat and cool. Whisk in the eggs, then switch to a wooden spoon to stir in your pecans. Pour the mixture into the pretzel crust and bake for 50 minutes. Cool the pie completely before serving.

1¼ cups salted pretzel crumbs (from 5 ounces pretzels)

2 tablespoons all-purpose flour

3 tablespoons granulated sugar

7 tablespoons unsalted butter, melted, plus 6 tablespoons, cut into pieces

1 cup firmly packed dark brown sugar

1 cup light corn syrup

1 tablespoon flaky sea salt (preferably Maldon)

3 large eggs, lightly beaten

2 cups chopped pecans

INGREDIENT NOTE

I like to use a flaky sea salt like Maldon, which has a more intense flavor than if you use a kosher or table salt. You'll taste the difference.

COOKING TIP

This pie can be made a day ahead. In fact, you want to prepare the pie with enough time for it to cool and set up. If not completely cool, pecan pies can be runny.

JACK'S FAVORITE BLONDIES

Makes two dozen 2-inch blondies

Prep time: 10 minutes
Cook time: 40 minutes

When I was growing up, my Great Aunt Glyniss made blondies every year at Thanksgiving. They've been everybody's favorite in this family at some point or another, and right now they're Jack's. See, he doesn't like chocolate, which kind of limits the number of baked goodies we can treat him to. But Great Aunt Glyniss's recipe seems to do the trick. It's not too sweet, but the toffee combined with the toasted pecans offers a buttery and nutty flavor that my son really enjoys.

3/4 cup (1 1/2 sticks) unsalted butter

2 1/4 cups firmly packed light brown sugar

2 cups all-purpose flour

2 teaspoons baking powder

3/4 teaspoon kosher salt

2 large eggs

2 teaspoons pure vanilla extract

1 cup toffee pieces

3/4 cup toasted pecans, chopped

Preheat the oven to 350°F. Adjust the racks to the center of the oven.

Line a 13 by 9-inch baking pan with foil, leaving a 2-inch overhang for easy removal after baking. Spray the foil lining with nonstick baking spray.

Melt the butter in a large saucepan over medium-high heat. Once it's melted, stir in the brown sugar and cook, stirring, until it's all combined. Remove the mixture from the heat and allow it to cool for 5 minutes. Meanwhile, whisk together the flour, baking powder, and salt in a medium bowl.

Stir the eggs into the cooled sugar and butter mixture one at a time, until they're well incorporated. Stir in the vanilla, and then add the flour mixture to the saucepan, mixing to combine. With a rubber spatula, fold in the toffee and chopped pecans.

Spread the batter in the prepared pan. Bake until golden brown and a toothpick inserted into the center comes out clean, 35 to 40 minutes. Let cool for 30 minutes. Using the overhanging foil, remove the blondies from the pan and slice them into 24 squares.

SUMMER STRAWBERRY OAT CRISP

Serves 6

Prep time: 15 minutes
Cook time: 30 minutes

When strawberry season arrives in the South, I pack up the family and drive to this beautiful place called Ottawa Farms, just a short drive outside of Savannah. The 700-acre farm has been around since 1878 and hosts an annual Strawberry Festival complete with music, pig races, a corn maze, cow train rides and an alligator show—I'm telling you, this is real country fun. We never miss the festival—or its trademark strawberry ice cream—but we also visit the farm all through the spring to pick berries. When we have more strawberries than we can use, we freeze them so we can warm up to this sweet and crunchy summery dessert in the fall and winter months.

2 pounds strawberries, hulled and halved (quartered if very large)

1/2 cup granulated sugar

3 tablespoons all-purpose flour

1 tablespoon lemon juice

1/8 teaspoon kosher salt

OAT TOPPING

1 cup old-fashioned oats

1/4 cup all-purpose flour

1/2 cup firmly packed light brown sugar

6 tablespoons unsalted butter, at room temperature

1/2 cup shelled roasted and salted pistachios, chopped

good vanilla ice cream or Homemade Whipped Cream (page 209)

Preheat your oven to 350°F. Spray a 1½-quart square baking dish with some nonstick baking spray.

In a large bowl, toss together the strawberries, sugar, flour, lemon juice, and salt, then spread the mixture in the prepared baking dish.

In a medium bowl, combine the oats, flour, brown sugar, butter, and pistachios, crumbling it all together with your hands. Evenly sprinkle the oat topping over the berries, then pop the baking dish in the oven and bake for 30 minutes, until the strawberries are soft, the filling is bubbling, and the topping is lightly golden.

Let the crisp cool for 30 minutes to allow the filling to thicken up. Serve it with a big ol' scoop of vanilla ice cream or whipped cream on top.

CRACKLY OATMEAL COOKIES

Makes 4 dozen cookies

Prep time: 10 minutes
Cook time: 15 minutes

The world is divided into two kinds of people—those who like their cookies chewy and those who like them crisp. I definitely fall into the former category. This cookie puffs up during baking and then falls as it cools, giving the tops a nice crackled appearance, while staying perfectly gooey on the inside.

$1/2$ cup (1 stick) unsalted butter, at room temperature

$1/2$ cup vegetable shortening

$1^1/2$ cups firmly packed light brown sugar

$1/2$ cup granulated sugar

2 large eggs

2 teaspoons pure vanilla extract

2 cups all-purpose flour

1 teaspoon baking soda

1 teaspoon ground cinnamon

$3/4$ teaspoon kosher salt

$2^1/2$ cups quick-cooking oats

$1/2$ cup raisins

SUGAR AND CINNAMON TOPPING

$1/2$ cup granulated sugar

1 teaspoon ground cinnamon

Preheat the oven to 350°F with the racks in the center.

Combine the butter, shortening, and both sugars in the bowl of a standing mixer fitted with a paddle attachment. Beat on medium-high speed until fluffy, about 5 minutes. Add the eggs, one at a time, beating well after each, then beat in the vanilla.

In a medium bowl, combine the flour, baking soda, cinnamon, and salt. Gradually add the dry ingredients to the wet ones, beating until combined. Using a rubber spatula, fold in the oats and raisins.

To make the topping, combine the sugar and cinnamon in a medium bowl. Roll the dough into golf-ball–size balls. Gently roll the balls through the sugar and cinnamon mixture. Place the cookies on a sheet tray, leaving 2 inches of space between each ball of dough. Bake the cookies for 12 to 14 minutes, until they're lightly golden.

Let the cookies cool on the pan for 2 minutes. Remove from the pan, and cool completely on wire racks.

LEMON SHORTBREAD COOKIES

Makes 4 dozen cookies

Prep time: 10 minutes (plus 1 hour chilling time)
Cook time: 20 minutes

Shortbread is one of those rare things that both kids and adults love. There aren't a lot of bells and whistles to this crumbly cookie—it's just a straight-up buttery biscuit that melts in your mouth. The addition of the lemon and the sanding sugar gives it something special without tampering with its timeless goodness.

1 cup (2 sticks) unsalted butter, at room temperature

1 cup confectioners' sugar

2 cups all-purpose flour

$^3/_4$ teaspoon kosher salt

1 tablespoon lemon zest (from 1 large lemon)

1 tablespoon lemon juice

pale yellow sanding sugar (optional)

Put the butter and confectioners' sugar in the bowl of a standing mixer fitted with a paddle attachment. Beat until light and fluffy, about 5 minutes, scraping down the sides of the bowl with a rubber spatula once or twice.

In a medium bowl, whisk together the flour, salt, and lemon zest. While the mixer is running, add half of the flour mixture to the creamed butter by large scoopfuls. Once the flour is incorporated, squeeze in the lemon juice, then add the remaining half of the flour mixture. The dough should stick together when pinched.

Set a large piece of wax paper in front of you. Place the dough on the center of the paper and form it into a log about 12 inches long. Roll the dough up in the paper, making a square log shape, and twist the ends of the paper to secure. Chill in the refrigerator for 1 hour.

Preheat the oven to 350°F. Then line a sheet tray with parchment paper.

Cut the chilled dough into $^1/_4$-inch-thick slices and place them on the prepared sheet tray, about 1 inch apart. Sprinkle the cookies with sanding sugar, if you like. Bake for 18 to 20 minutes, until the cookies are light golden brown around the edges. Cool them for 5 minutes on the sheet tray then remove to a wire rack to cool completely.

FRESH FRUIT AMBROSIA WITH SHREDDED COCONUT

Serves 6

Prep time: 15 minutes
Cook time: 10 minutes

Momma had a plastic storage container that magically appeared at Christmas when she made her ambrosia salad. It should've held enough salad to feed twenty people, but it only fed the four of us because we loved it so much. A lot of folks add whipped topping, mayonnaise or marshmallows to their salad, but I like how Mom always kept it clean and simple: nothing but heaping spoonfuls of fruit and coconut.

1/2 cup sweetened and shredded coconut

1/2 cup roughly chopped pecans

3 navel oranges, peeled and segmented

2 medium blood oranges, peeled and segmented

1 medium ruby red grapefruit, peeled and segmented

1/2 medium ripe pineapple, peeled, cored, and diced

1/2 cup jarred maraschino cherries, drained and sliced in half

1 medium banana, peeled and sliced

Preheat the oven to 350°F.

Spread the coconut and pecans out on a sheet tray and toast them in the oven until the coconut is golden brown, about 7 minutes. Transfer to a plate to cool.

Toss the navel and blood oranges, grapefruit, pineapple, cherries, and banana together in a large bowl. Scoop up any juice that you may have lost on your work surface from segmenting the citrus and add it to the bowl as well. Sprinkle in the coconut and pecans and toss it all together.

COOKING TIPS

You can make this up to a day ahead of time. Just leave out the banana until right before you serve, otherwise it will turn brown and soften. Then sprinkle with toasted coconut—you don't want to lose that crunch. Feel free to thinly slice the citrus into rounds instead of segmenting.

YES, A JELLY SALAD

Serves 6 to 8

Prep time: 10 minutes
Cook time: 10 minutes (plus
4 hours chilling time)

A cookbook coming out of the South without a jelly salad would be like Saturday morning without cartoons. Total blasphemy. The only thing worse would be if you've never actually had a jelly salad.

Calling this dish a "salad" is a bit of a misnomer. It's really an amped-up strawberry cheesecake, but I can't ever wait until after the meal to enjoy it, so I insist on making it something we serve alongside the entrée. Brooke makes jelly salad every year at Christmastime and brings it to Mom's house. As a testament to how good it is, I always cut back on my mom's dishes because I'm saving room for that salad. (But you didn't hear that from me.)

CRUST
8 ounces salted pretzels
10 tablespoons unsalted butter, melted
1/4 cup sugar

1 package (8 ounces) cream cheese, at room temperature
3/4 cup sugar
1 container (8 ounces) whipped topping, thawed
1 1/2 pounds fresh strawberries, hulled and sliced
1 package (6 ounces) strawberry gelatin
2 cups boiling water
2 cups cold water

Preheat the oven to 350°F. Spray a 13 by 9-inch baking pan with nonstick baking spray.

Put the pretzels in the bowl of a food processor and buzz them until you're left with chunky crumbs. You'll need 2 cups of the crushed pretzels for the crust.

In a medium bowl, mix together the pretzels, melted butter, and sugar. Firmly press the pretzel mixture into the bottom of the prepared pan and bake for 10 minutes. Allow the crust to cool completely, about 30 minutes.

Add the cream cheese to a standing mixer fitted with a whisk attachment and beat until nice and smooth. Sprinkle in the sugar and beat again until light and fluffy, about 3 minutes. With a rubber spatula, fold in the whipped topping and spread it over the cooled crust, making sure to seal all the edges. Layer the sliced strawberries on top and place in the refrigerator to chill for 1 hour.

Place the gelatin in a medium bowl and pour the boiling water over it, stirring to dissolve. Stir in the cold water. Gently pour the gelatin over the chilled salad. Refrigerate until the salad is completely set and chilled, about 4 hours.

APPLE CINNAMON STREUSEL CAKE

Serves 8

Prep time: 15 minutes
Cook time: 50 minutes

I'm not a real big dessert guy, but the ones that I lean toward always involve some kind of baked fruit. This soft, moist apple cake has a sweet and crunchy topping that reminds me of cinnamon toast, only better—like six tablespoons of butter better. I like to use Honeycrisp apples, but any sweet, crisp apple will do.

Preheat the oven to 350°F. Spray an 8 by 8-inch baking dish with nonstick baking spray.

First make the streusel: In a medium bowl, combine the brown sugar, flour, cinnamon, and salt, whisking together until well blended. Use a fork to cut in the butter, then switch to your fingers to really crumble the streusel all together. Once it's all combined, stir in the walnuts. Pinch together some of the topping to create some large crumbles for varying texture. Set aside the topping while you make the cake.

In a second medium bowl, whisk together the flour, baking powder, cinnamon, allspice, and salt.

In the bowl of a standing mixer fitted with a whisk attachment, add the butter and sugar and beat until the mixture is light and fluffy, about 5 minutes. With a rubber spatula, scrape down to the bottom of the bowl halfway through beating to ensure it's all coming together. Beat in the eggs, one at a time, making sure the first is well blended before adding the second, then beat in the sour cream and vanilla. Add the flour mixture by scoopfuls and mix until well incorporated. Turn the mixer off and stir in the diced apples. Your batter should be thick.

Pour the batter into the pan, smooth the top, and sprinkle with the streusel. Bake for 50 to 55 minutes, until a toothpick inserted into the center comes out clean. Leave to cool for about 30 minutes before serving.

STREUSEL

1/3 cup firmly packed light brown sugar

1/3 cup all-purpose flour

1 teaspoon ground cinnamon

1/4 teaspoon kosher salt

6 tablespoons unsalted butter, chilled and cut into small cubes

1/2 cup chopped walnuts

1 1/2 cups all-purpose flour

1 teaspoon baking powder

1 teaspoon ground cinnamon

1/2 teaspoon allspice

1/2 teaspoon kosher salt

1/2 cup (1 stick) unsalted butter, at room temperature

3/4 cup sugar

2 large eggs, at room temperature

3/4 cup sour cream

1 teaspoon pure vanilla extract

2 cups cored, peeled, and diced apples (1 1/2 medium Honeycrisp or other sweet, crisp apples)

THE BEST LEMON TART

Serves 8

Prep time: 20 minutes
Cook time: 50 minutes

There may be lots of different tarts in the world, but to me there's just a lemon tart. That's why it's "the best."

This sweet and citrusy dessert is perfect when you want a lot of bang for your buck. The freshly squeezed lemon juice paired with a nutty almond crust packs flavor into every bite. You won't need a big slice to get the full effect, but you will ask for another just because it's that good.

CRUST

¹/₄ cup blanched slivered almonds

1¹/₄ cups all-purpose flour, plus more for dusting

¹/₂ cup confectioners' sugar

¹/₄ teaspoon kosher salt

10 tablespoons unsalted butter, chilled and sliced

1 large egg, lightly beaten

LEMON CURD

1¹/₄ cups granulated sugar

³/₄ cup freshly squeezed lemon juice (from 4 to 5 lemons)

¹/₄ teaspoon kosher salt

4 large eggs plus 1 large yolk

6 tablespoons unsalted butter, chilled and sliced

confectioners' sugar for serving (optional)

To make the crust, toast the almonds in a small dry skillet over medium heat, stirring, until just slightly blond, about 3 minutes. Transfer to a plate to cool completely.

Add the flour, confectioners' sugar, and salt to a food processor and pulse a few times to mix and break up any lumps in the sugar. Add the cooled almonds and pulse again for 30 seconds, until they are broken up. Add the butter and pulse until the dough forms small clumps. Add the beaten egg and pulse in long increments until the dough comes together, bunched up into a few balls.

Lightly dust your work surface with flour. Use nonstick baking spray to prepare a 9-inch tart pan with a removable bottom. Transfer the dough to the work surface. Lightly knead it a few times to incorporate all the dry ingredients, and then form it into a flat disk. Press the dough into the bottom of the prepared tart pan and up the sides. Chill for 30 minutes in the freezer. Preheat the oven to 350°F.

Once chilled, remove the tart from the freezer and place it on a baking sheet. With a fork, prick the bottom of the tart all over to prevent the dough from puffing while it bakes. Line the tart with parchment paper and place pie weights on top (dried beans will work in a pinch). Bake the crust for 25 minutes. Remove the tart from the oven, remove the parchment and pie weights, and bake the crust for 2 more minutes until lightly golden. (If the crust has puffed during baking, press it back down with the back of a spoon.)

Meanwhile, make the lemon curd: In a heavy-bottomed medium saucepan, whisk together the granulated sugar, lemon juice, salt, and eggs. Turn the heat to medium and cook, while stirring, until the curd is thick, about 8 minutes. (If you're worried about how to tell whether the curd is fully cooked, it's done when it reaches 170°F.) Whisk in the butter, piece by piece; the curd will loosen up slightly. Pour the mixture into a large measuring cup.

Carefully pour the lemon curd into the crust. (Do not overfill.) Bake the tart until the custard is set, about 10 minutes. Remove the tart from the oven and let it cool completely in the pan. Remove the sides from the tart pan and slice the tart. Sprinkle with confectioners' sugar to serve.

Any recipe where ice cream functions as a garnish has got to be good.

Peach cobbler has been a staple at our restaurant for more than twenty-five years. One day, I decided to shake things up by throwing in some blackberries and it turned out that we all really liked those two flavors together. Now this is my family's go-to cobbler.

PEACH AND BLACKBERRY COBBLER

Serves 6 to 8

Prep time: 15 minutes
Cook time: 55 minutes

Preheat the oven to 350°F. Adjust the rack to the center of your oven.

Add the butter to a 3-quart baking dish and place it in the oven just until the butter melts. Then quickly remove from the oven and set aside.

In a medium saucepan, combine the peaches, blackberries, 1 cup of the sugar, and the water and mix well. Bring the mixture to a boil, reduce the heat to a simmer, and cook for 10 minutes, until the peaches and berries are soft and the liquid is syrupy.

In a medium bowl, whisk together the flour, baking powder, salt, and remaining 1 cup sugar. Slowly whisk in the milk and cinnamon, if using, mixing until smooth. Pour the batter over the butter in the baking dish, and then spoon the fruit and syrup on top. Bake for 45 minutes. Serve warm with a big scoop of vanilla ice cream.

INGREDIENT NOTE

I recommend fresh, but you can also use frozen fruit as well. I like baking with yellow peaches because they are slightly less sweet than white peaches and have a more intense flavor.

½ cup (1 stick) unsalted butter, melted

4 peaches, peeled, pitted and sliced (about 1½ pounds)

6 ounces fresh blackberries (1½ cups)

2 cups sugar

½ cup water

1½ cups all-purpose flour

2¼ teaspoons baking powder

½ teaspoon kosher salt

1¼ cups whole milk

½ teaspoon ground cinnamon (optional)

"ARE YOU THIRSTY? WANT A SNACK?"

"Are you thirsty? Want a snack?"

When I became a parent, there was so much that I wasn't prepared for—things that only experience can teach you, like the incredible lengths you'll be willing to go to to get your child to sleep. I wore a path around the house, circling it with a baby in my arms, singing the only verse to "Hush, Little Baby" that I knew, over and over and over again.

It's this relentless repetition that surprised me the most.

As Jack has gotten older, I've stopped walking in circles and, to Brooke's relief, learned to offer more than just the "mockingbird," but I still repeat myself on a daily—no, hourly—basis. "Do you need to use the bathroom?" "Please don't run with scissors." "Please don't paint _____." (Insert "the sofa," "the dog," or "your brother.") And, my personal favorite, "Are you thirsty? Do you want a snack?"

I've discovered that kids don't announce that they're hungry or thirsty until they're borderline starving or dehydrated, at which point they lose the ability to use their words and instead resort to undesirable, nonverbal cues such as crying or fainting. To avoid this scenario, I find myself repeatedly offering my boys satisfying snacks and drinks like the homemade Cheesy Cheddar Puffs and fresh-squeezed Savannah Minted Lemonade included in this chapter.

I'd like to think I'm able to separate my roles as parent and host, but the truth is, there's some overlap. I've never had a guest in my home ask for something to eat or drink: I don't give them the chance. As soon as you cross our threshold, you're going to be bombarded with offers of food and drink until you finally accept. Southerners are just as relentless as they are hospitable, y'all.

Sweet tea and candied pecans are certainly tradition around here, but I also like to offer guests something outside the Southern sphere, so to speak. My recipes for candied orange peels, biscuits, and even collard wontons are easy to do and leave a big impression. Many of the drinks in this chapter incorporate fresh fruits and herbs, and all of the adult drinks that include liquor can be modified for children who want to feel grown up. Likewise, the kid-friendly drinks can be easily dressed up with a jigger of this or that. In the end, nobody goes hungry or thirsty on my watch.

I just can't promise that the dog won't get painted.

SAVANNAH MINTED LEMONADE

Serves 12

Prep time: 10 minutes
Cook time: 5 minutes

There's no better way to quench your thirst in the summer than a tall glass of freshly squeezed lemonade packed with ice. I've got a Meyer lemon tree in the yard with these big, beautiful lemons that come in all at once, so I make a point of squeezing pitchers full of them when that happens. The cool hint of mint makes this lemonade even more refreshing—and it adds some nice color. It's the perfect porch drink.

8 cups cold water

2 cups sugar

1 cup loosely packed fresh mint leaves, plus more for garnish

2 cups freshly squeezed lemon juice (from 9 or 10 lemons), plus additional lemon rounds for serving (optional)

In a medium saucepan, combine 2 cups of the water, the sugar, and mint, gently twisting the leaves to release the essential oils. Turn the heat to medium-high and bring to a boil, stirring until the sugar dissolves. Reduce the heat and simmer for 2 minutes, then remove from the heat and cool completely, letting the mint steep in the hot syrup.

Strain the sugar syrup into a pitcher, discarding your mint leaves. Stir in the lemon juice and remaining 6 cups cold water. Tear up a few fresh mint leaves and add them to the pitcher. Refrigerate until chilled. Serve your lemonade in tall, ice-filled glasses garnished with mint leaves and lemon rounds, if you like.

COOKING TIP

Before squeezing the lemons, give 'em a roll on the countertop to help release the juice.

STRAWBERRY SIPPER

Serves 5

Prep time: 15 minutes (plus 1 hour marinatin')
Cook time: zero

Whenever Jack sees adults drinking colorful cocktails with paper umbrellas and fruit garnish, he thinks he's missing out. So, at restaurants we sometimes order him a classic Shirley Temple—soda water and cherry juice with a maraschino cherry floating on top. It's good, but it doesn't hold a candle to this combination of strawberries, limes, and mint. Because the garnish is really what makes a drink seem adult to Jack, this Strawberry Sipper is a win-win for both of us: He gets to enjoy a fresh fruit "mocktail," and I can enjoy a grown-up version by adding some tequila.

4 quarts fresh strawberries, hulled and quartered

juice of 3 limes (about 6 tablespoons)

20 fresh mint leaves, plus additional sprigs for serving

1/3 cup superfine sugar

8 ounces tequila (optional)

club soda

Combine the strawberries, lime juice, mint, and sugar in a blender and pulse to create a chunky puree. Transfer to a small glass pitcher and stir in the tequila, if using. Place in the refrigerator for 1 hour, until well chilled and the flavors have had a chance to marry together (if time allows, sometimes we can't wait!).

Pour about 1/2 cup of the strawberry mixture over each ice-filled rocks glass, top with club soda, and give a little stir. Garnish each drink with a mint sprig.

INGREDIENT NOTE

For an interesting variation on this sipper, use basil in place of the mint and vodka in place of the tequila.

What makes this a "Savannah" lemonade? The two cups of sugar. If you ever have our sweet tea, you'll understand.

When you have friends coming over, this is a great make-ahead drink recipe because you don't have to muddle the drinks one by one.

FROZEN GEORGIA PEACH MARGARITA

Makes 6 drinks

Prep time: 5 minutes
Cook time: zero

Texans know a thing or two about cattle ranching and drilling for oil, but they also have a long and loving relationship with beer. So, I guess it shouldn't have surprised me when a friend of mine from there made me a "Texas Margarita" with, you guessed it, beer. It adds another layer of flavor that partners well with the bite of the limeade and tequila. I'm willing to give credit where it's due, but as soon as I added peaches, this margarita crossed into Georgia territory.

1 cup tequila

1 can (6 ounces) limeade concentrate, thawed but still chilled

1 cup beer

1 bag (16 ounces) frozen peaches

1 cup ice cubes

coarse salt (optional)

Combine all of the ingredients in a blender (except the salt, of course) and blend until smooth. Serve your margaritas in salt-rimmed glasses, if desired.

INGREDIENT NOTE

You can go ahead and use the whole can of limeade if you prefer your margaritas sweeter.

PARTY PUNCH

Serves 15

Prep time: 5 minutes (plus freezing time)
Cook time: zero

Punch is an easy and cost-effective alternative to made-to-order cocktails when you have a festive gathering. The fresh fruit ice ring adds an element of fun to the punch that's both pretty and functional— it keeps your drink cold without watering it down.

2 limes, sliced

2 pints fresh raspberries

1 quart pomegranate juice

1 bottle (2 liters) ginger ale, chilled

1 bottle (59 ounces) limeade, chilled ($7^1/_2$ cups)

2 to 3 bottles (750 milliliters) prosecco (optional)

First make your ice ring: Place the sliced limes and raspberries on the bottom of a Bundt pan. Cover the fruit with cold water by 4 inches. Freeze overnight until the ice forms a solid ring.

When you're ready to serve, combine the pomegranate juice, ginger ale, and limeade in a 2-gallon punch bowl. To unmold the ice ring, run the bottom side of the pan under warm water to loosen it. Carefully place the ice ring in the punch bowl, fruit side up.

Offer the bottles of chilled prosecco next to the punch, if the adults want to top off their drinks.

PEPPERMINT HOT COCOA

Serves 4

Prep time: 10 minutes
Cook time: 10 minutes

Hot cocoa is such a satisfying drink, but part of what makes it so magical is the fact that we don't have it every day. It's a treat we get to enjoy on a cold winter's afternoon when nothing else will warm us, or our spirits. The peppermint gives my recipe a little something extra—a festive twist on tradition—and a generous heap of homemade whipped cream beats out chewy marshmallows every time.

1 pint whole milk

1 pint half-and-half

8 ounces good-quality milk chocolate chips (1 heaping cup)

16 round hard peppermint candies (3 ounces), crushed, plus 4 more crushed candies for serving

Homemade Whipped Cream for serving (page 209)

In a large saucepan over medium heat, heat the milk and half-and-half. Once it's warm, add the chocolate and crushed peppermints and whisk until the chocolate is melted and the peppermint is dissolved, about 5 minutes. Serve the cocoa in mugs and top each with a big dollop of whipped cream and a sprinkle of the extra crushed peppermint.

MULLED CIDER

Serves 4

Prep time: 5 minutes
Cook time: 25 minutes

If the temperature drops to a frigid 49°F, adults should feel free to add a shot of bourbon.

The South can get really cold in the winter—like 50 degrees. And while that might sound like a beach day to those living in the Northeast, you've got to understand that more than two decades of sunshine can change a man. To warm up, Brooke and I make a batch of this spicy and fragrant mulled cider that the boys also can enjoy when they need to defrost.

5 cups apple cider

2 cinnamon sticks

1 (2-inch) piece fresh ginger, sliced into rounds

1 star anise

3 (2-inch) strips lemon peel

$1/8$ teaspoon ground cloves

Combine all of your ingredients in a large saucepan over medium-high heat. Bring up to a boil, then reduce the heat to a low simmer, and gently simmer for 20 minutes. Remove from the heat and steep for 5 minutes. Serve the cider in mugs and get cozy.

THE DEEN FAMILY EGGNOG

Serves 15

Prep time: 25 minutes (plus chilling time)
Cook time: zero

My grandmother Hiers made eggnog every year at Christma—a family tradition my mom kept up with. We kids were so fascinated by it because it looked so delicious—all thick and creamy, like what I imagined a sweet-cream-butter milk shake would look like. But we could never drink any 'cause, just like my grandmother, Momma put bourbon in it. It's not an everyday drink; it's not even an every-so-often drink. But in my family, it's the holiday drink of choice.

6 large eggs, separated

$^3/_4$ cup sugar

1 quart whole milk

1 cup bourbon (optional)

1 pint heavy cream

1 tablespoon pure vanilla extract

freshly grated nutmeg for serving

Put the egg yolks in the bowl of a standing mixer fitted with the whisk attachment and beat until combined. While beating, slowly add $^1/_2$ cup of the sugar to the egg yolks and continue beating until the mixture is thick and light yellow in color, about 4 minutes. Whisk in the milk and, if using, the bourbon.

In a second bowl, beat the egg whites until they're frothy, then slowly add the remaining $^1/_4$ cup sugar, beating until stiff peaks appear.

In a third bowl, beat the heavy cream and vanilla together until stiff peaks appear, then gently fold into the eggnog. Chill in the refrigerator for 2 to 4 hours before serving with freshly grated nutmeg, to taste.

INGREDIENT NOTE

If you like the flavor of bourbon but not the fuzzy head that comes with it, you can exchange it for a tablespoon of rum extract.

At one of our favorite bakeries here in town, Back in the Day Bakery, owners Cheryl and Griff Day make these incredible biscuits with bacon cooked into them, except they call them "biscones." For somebody like me from South Georgia, anything that looks like a biscuit and tastes like a biscuit is a *biscuit*. The end. This recipe is inspired by Back in the Day's.

BACON CHEDDAR BISCUITS

Makes 12 biscuits

Prep time: 20 minutes
Cook time: 15 minutes

Preheat the oven to 400°F and line a sheet tray with parchment.

In a large skillet, cook your bacon over medium-high heat until crisp. Remove it with a slotted spoon to a paper towel–lined plate to cool. Set aside 1 tablespoon of the bacon drippings in a small bowl.

In a large bowl, whisk together the flour, baking powder, sugar, salt, baking soda, green onion, and cooled bacon. Using a fork, cut the butter into the dry ingredients until the mixture looks like coarse crumbs, then stir in the cheese.

Dig a well in the center of your flour and slowly stir in the buttermilk and reserved bacon drippings, just until the dough is sticky but still a bit crumbly on the bottom of your bowl. Dust your work surface with some flour and dump the dough onto your surface and knead three or four times until all the loose crumbs come together. Pat into a rough round shape with your hands and press the dough to a 3/4-inch thickness. With a 2 1/4-inch-round biscuit cutter, cut out twelve biscuits, making sure you do not twist.

Place the biscuits on the prepared baking sheet, allowing 2 inches of space between each one. Brush the tops with some buttermilk. Bake the biscuits for 15 minutes, until the tops are lightly golden, rotating the pan halfway through baking.

8 ounces bacon, chopped

1 3/4 cups all-purpose flour, plus more for dusting

1 1/2 teaspoons baking powder

1 teaspoon sugar

1/2 teaspoon kosher salt

1/2 teaspoon baking soda

1 green onion, thinly sliced

4 tablespoons unsalted butter, chilled and cut into cubes

3/4 cup grated cheddar cheese

3/4 cup buttermilk, plus more for brushing

CORNY CORNBREAD

Serves 6 to 8

Prep time: 15 minutes
Cook time: 25 minutes

Cornbread without actual kernels of corn is like an apple pie without the apples—I just don't get it. But it's amazing to me how often cornmeal passes for "corn" in many cornbread recipes. Not this one. I'm husking corn from the actual cob to give this recipe some authenticity. The result is a dense, moist cornbread that's the perfect pairing for Chili (page 42), Black-eyed Peas (page 199), or any other savory Southern dish.

6 tablespoons butter

1 ear of corn, husked and kernels removed from the cob

3 green onions, sliced

kosher salt and freshly ground black pepper

1 cup yellow cornmeal

1 cup all-purpose flour

2 tablespoons sugar

1½ teaspoons baking powder

½ teaspoon baking soda

1 cup grated cheddar cheese

1½ cups buttermilk

2 large eggs, lightly beaten

Preheat your oven to 425°F and adjust the rack to the center of the oven. Spray an 8 by 8-inch baking dish with nonstick baking spray.

In a large skillet, heat the butter until melted and foamy. Add the corn kernels and green onions and sauté over medium-high heat until the corn is soft, about 2 minutes. Season with a nice hit of salt and pepper, then remove from the heat and set aside.

In a large bowl, whisk together the cornmeal, flour, sugar, baking powder, baking soda, and ½ teaspoon salt. Add the cheese and toss to combine with your hands. Transfer the sautéed corn mixture to a separate large bowl, using a rubber spatula to scrape all the butter and bits into the bowl. Add the buttermilk and eggs and stir to combine.

Make a well in the center of the dry ingredients, pour the buttermilk-corn mixture into the well, then stir until just combined.

Pour the batter into your prepared baking dish and bake for 30 to 35 minutes, or until a toothpick inserted in the center of the bread comes out clean. Allow the cornbread to cool before serving it up.

COLLARD GREEN WONTONS

Serves 8 to 10

Prep time: 25 minutes
Cook time: 35 minutes (plus frying time)

We developed this recipe at the restaurant and loved it so much we served these wontons at Mom's wedding reception. Besides being really pretty, they bring together two otherwise distinct cultures—the Far East and Down South—in an interesting and tasty way, marrying a flaky shell with creamy bacon-infused greens on the inside. It's a proven winner at the restaurant and a recipe you can easily bring to your next party.

8 ounces collard greens

kosher salt and freshly ground black pepper

1 dried chile pepper

4 slices bacon, chopped

$\frac{1}{2}$ medium Vidalia onion (or other sweet onion), finely chopped

4 ounces goat cheese, softened

1 package (17 ounces) wonton wrappers

peanut oil for frying

To prepare the collards, strip the green leaves off the stems and toss them into a clean sink filled with cold water. Agitate the water with your hands to make sure the greens get clean. Pile the leaves up, roll them into a cigar, and slice into 1/2-inch-thick strips.

Bring a large Dutch oven of salted water plus the chile pepper to a boil. Add the greens and simmer for 20 to 25 minutes, until tender. Remove your collards with a slotted spoon to a bowl to cool. Discard the chile pepper. Once cool, gently squeeze all the excess liquid from the collards.

In a large skillet over medium heat, cook the bacon for 1 to 2 minutes, until it's rendered enough fat to cook the onion. Add the onion and sauté until tender and soft and the bacon is crisp, 4 to 5 minutes. Season with a pinch of salt and lots of black pepper. Transfer the bacon and onion to the bowl with the collard greens to cool.

To make the filling, put the goat cheese and collard green mixture in a food processor and blend until well combined.

To assemble the wontons, add 1 heaping teaspoon of the filling to the center of a wonton wrapper. Wet the edges of the wrapper with your finger, then fold the wrapper over and press to seal the edges, making sure to press out any air. Repeat with the remaining filling and wontons; you should have about 40 wontons total.

To cook the wontons, heat 2 inches of oil in a high-sided skillet until it reaches 375°F on a deep-frying thermometer. Fry the wontons in batches until they're golden brown and crisp, about 2 minutes. Drain on a paper towel–lined sheet tray. The filling will be piping hot so let the wontons cool for a few minutes before serving.

INGREDIENT NOTE

Fresh out of wonton wrappers? You can also serve the filling with crackers as an unexpected collard green dip.

CHEESY CHEDDAR PUFFS

Makes 26 to 30

Prep time: 5 minutes
Cook time: 35 minutes

These are best served warm and with drinks. Boxed juice or bottled beer; it's your call.

Cheese straws are really big around here—they're the Southern equivalent of beer nuts. For this recipe, I've reinvented them as "puffs" so they look super kid-friendly (especially in a lunch box) but have a grown-up bite to 'em. That's cayenne pepper, but you can back off on that if your kids are, well, babies.

1 cup whole milk

1/2 cup (1 stick) butter, chilled and cut into chunks

2 teaspoons kosher salt

1/2 teaspoon freshly ground black pepper

1 cup all-purpose flour

pinch cayenne pepper

4 large eggs, at room temperature

1 1/4 cups grated sharp cheddar cheese

Preheat the oven to 375°F. Line two sheet trays with parchment paper or silicone baking mats and lightly coat with nonstick baking spray.

In a large saucepan over medium heat, combine the milk, butter, salt and pepper, stirring, until the butter is fully melted. Sprinkle in the flour and cayenne, and stir vigorously with a wooden spoon until the dough comes together in the bottom of the pot, moves away from the sides of the pan, and looks shiny and smooth, about 2 minutes. Transfer the dough to the bowl of a stand mixer fitted with the whisk attachment and cool for 1 minute.

Beat in the eggs, one at a time, then add 1 cup cheese and beat until a smooth dough forms.

Drop the dough by tablespoons onto the prepared sheet tray, leaving about 2 inches of space between each ball. Sprinkle with the remaining 1/4 cup cheese.

Bake for 30 minutes, rotating the pans halfway through, until puffed and golden brown. Serve 'em up warm.

COOKING TIPS

In order to work quickly, it's best to prepare and measure all of your ingredients before starting this recipe. Jack loves to help me make these puffs because, like cookies, it's a drop-dough recipe.

CANDIED ORANGE PEEL

Makes 1 cup

Prep time: 10 minutes
Cook time: 55 minutes

Everyone loves candy, but many people are turned off by the idea of fussing around with thermometers, molds, and scorching-hot syrups that rival molten lava. But this is not that kind of candy. It's a really easy recipe that I picked up when I was a kid and have made a million times since.

🥄 COOKING TIP

Around the holidays, I like to put these candied peels out in little dishes, but they also make for a nice garnish on just about any dessert—after all, even the most decadent chocolate torte can handle a little dressing up.

2 navel oranges
1 cup sugar
3/4 cup water

Line a sheet tray with parchment paper. Use a vegetable peeler to remove the peels from the oranges. Try to remove just the peel and not too much of the bitter white pith. Slice the peels into 1/4-inch-thick strips and toss them in a saucepan of cold water. Bring up to a boil, then reduce the heat to a simmer and cook for 10 minutes. Drain the peels and let 'em cool.

Add 3/4 cup of the sugar and the water to the same saucepan and bring to a boil, all the while stirring to dissolve the sugar. Turn the heat to low, add the peels, and simmer them gently for 45 minutes, stirring occasionally, until the mixture is very syrupy.

With tongs, transfer the peels to the prepared sheet tray, using the tongs to separate them if they've stuck together. (Don't use your hands, the zest will be real hot.) Cool the candied peels for 5 minutes. Sprinkle the remaining 1/4 cup sugar over the tops to coat. Let the peels dry for 30 minutes, then store them in an airtight container for up to 2 weeks.

Date Night With Old Sparky

Just to clarify, "Old Sparky" isn't Brooke's nickname for me—yet. It's what Southerners call the electric chair. See, we have this habit of making things sound better than they actually are. "Chitlins" for example, sound like cute, baby "chits," but they're actually fried pig intestines.

So, when I got to thinking about my favorite meal of all time, I asked myself the age-old question: If I was facing certain death, what would I want my last meal to be?

For some, this question is a bit like being asked to pick your favorite child. I enjoy so many different kinds of foods. If I didn't, I certainly wouldn't be where I am today, writing this book for y'all. Instead, I would've followed my dreams of becoming a writer of a different sort, and I'd probably be living on Mom's couch right now.

So how can I choose just one meal?

As it turns out, the answer, for me, is quite simple. And I don't even have to wait to be sentenced to death to enjoy it, because it's the same meal Momma makes every New Year's Day: fried pork chops, collard greens with corn dumplings, black-eyed peas, lacy hoecakes, and cane syrup and butter on white bread—it's the stuff Southern boys are made of.

A favorite meal transports us back in time. For some, it may be the dish they associate with a special moment, like an engagement or milestone birthday. For others, it's an incredible restaurant meal they enjoyed while vacationing in someplace memorable and magical, like New York City or Paris. For me, it's the traditional meal by which I greet each New Year and all of the possibilities it holds.

But because this is my last meal, I would make one revision: I would eat three times the amount I do every January 1st. Besides, I'll be gone long before heartburn sets in.

COLLARD GREENS WITH CORNMEAL DUMPLINGS

Serves 4 to 6

Prep time: 20 minutes
Cook time: 1 hour 45 minutes

It's a myth that collard greens have to be bathed in butter to taste good. In this recipe, they absorb their full flavor from the smoked wings. Plus, because they're rich in vitamins C and K, and soluble fiber, they're really nutritious. The cornmeal dumplings are just a bonus—golden nuggets nestled on a bed of greens.

2^1/$_2$ quarts water

12 ounces smoked turkey wings

1 tablespoon hot sauce

1 teaspoon kosher salt

2 tablespoons butter

1 pound collard greens (1 large bunch)

CORNMEAL DUMPLINGS

1 cup yellow cornmeal

1 cup all-purpose flour

1 tablespoon sugar

1 teaspoon kosher salt

1 cup cooking liquid (from the collards)

2 tablespoons butter, melted

1 large egg, lightly beaten

2 tablespoons minced Vidalia onion

1 tablespoon finely chopped fresh parsley

In a large Dutch oven over medium-high heat, combine the water, smoked wings, hot sauce, salt, and butter. Bring to a boil, then reduce to a simmer and cook for 1 hour.

Strip the leaves off the collard greens and toss them into a clean sink filled with cold water. Agitate the water with your hands to make sure the greens get clean. Pile the leaves up, roll into a cigar, and slice into ^{1}/$_2$-inch-thick strips. Add the greens to the pot with the wings and simmer for 20 minutes, stirring occasionally, until tender. In a small bowl, reserve 1 cup cooking liquid for your dumplings. Using tongs, remove the collards to a serving bowl and cover to keep warm. Discard the wings; set the broth aside.

To make the dumplings, in a medium bowl, whisk together the cornmeal, flour, sugar, and salt. Stir in the reserved cooking liquid, butter, egg, onion, and parsley.

Bring the reserved collard broth back up to a low simmer and carefully drop the dumpling batter into it, 1 tablespoon at a time. Gently shake the pot instead of stirring with a spoon so the dumplings won't fall apart. Simmer the dumplings lightly until cooked through, 20 to 25 minutes. Serve the collards and dumplings with some of the broth ladled over the top.

BLACK-EYED PEAS WITH HAM HOCKS

Serves 6

Prep time: 20 minutes
Cook time: 2 hours 25 minutes (plus
overnight soaking and chilling)

Ever heard of osso buco? That's the
fancy name Italians use for ham hock,
when really they should just call it
"black-eyed-peas seasoning."

I'm always shocked when I have customers who come into the restaurant and say they've never tasted black-eyed peas. Once they try them, they're always surprised by how incredible peas can taste. The secret ingredient here is the ham hock—it goes into all of our Southern-prepared vegetables, from collard greens to pole beans. It's where the flavor comes from. I don't care where you grew up, once you've enjoyed this traditional dish, you won't wait until you're south of the Mason-Dixon line to make it for yourself.

1 pound dried black-eyed peas

1 large ham hock (1 pound)

2 tablespoons olive oil

1 medium onion, chopped

kosher salt and freshly ground black pepper

3 cloves garlic, chopped

2 sprigs fresh thyme

1 bay leaf

1 small dried chile pepper

1 glug hot sauce, to taste

Pick through the black-eyed peas to remove and toss out any small stones or shriveled-up peas. Place the peas that passed inspection in a colander, rinse them well under cold water, then add them to a big bowl and cover with cold water. Cover the bowl with plastic wrap and let the peas sit and soak overnight.

Carefully cut the ham hock into three separate pieces, working around the bone. Put the ham hocks in a large Dutch oven and add enough cold water to cover plus 1 inch. Bring to a boil, then reduce to a moderate simmer and cook, uncovered, for 1½ hours, or until the ham hock is tender. Cool to room temperature, then store the ham stock with the ham hock in the fridge overnight.

The next day, heat a large pot over medium-high heat. Add the oil, and once hot, stir in the onion and sauté until softened, about 5 minutes. Season with salt and pepper, then stir in the garlic and sauté until fragrant, about 1 minute. Drain the peas and add them to the pot, along with the reserved ham hock and ham stock. Toss in the thyme, bay leaf, and chile pepper. Bring the mixture to a boil, then reduce to a low simmer and cook for 45 minutes, stirring on occasion. Transfer the ham hock to a cutting board to cool slightly. Once it's cool enough to handle, give the meat a rough chop and stir it back into the pot, discarding any bones. Taste for seasoning and adjust as necessary with salt, pepper, and a glug of hot sauce.

 COOKING TIP

These might seem a bit of work: Both the beans and the ham stock should be prepared the day before to allow for overnight soaking. But these wouldn't be real Southern black-eyed peas without ham hocks. Believe me, it's worth the effort!

MOMMA'S FRIED PORK CHOPS

Serves 4

Prep time: 5 minutes
Cook time: 10 minutes

This is a loosen-my-belt meal. I don't have it often, but when I do, I do it right.

Momma's fried pork chops are my favorite. The end.

2 cups canola oil
4 (1-inch-thick) bone-in pork chops (8 to 10 ounces each)
kosher salt and freshly ground black pepper
1 cup all-purpose flour

Line a sheet tray with paper towels. Pour the oil into a large, high-sided skillet; you want the oil to be about 1/2 inch deep. Heat the oil to 350°F over medium-high heat.

Season the pork chops on both sides with salt and pepper. Put the flour in a baking dish and season with salt and pepper, whisking until combined. Dredge the pork chops in the flour on both sides and shake off any excess. Carefully add the pork chops to the hot oil and cook for 5 minutes on each side until they're golden brown and cooked through. Once they come out of the skillet, drain them on the prepared sheet tray and season again with a little pinch of salt.

LACY HOECAKES

Serves 6

Prep time: 5 minutes
Cook time: 40 minutes

You wouldn't eat mashed potatoes without gravy; the same goes for hoecakes and cane syrup.

Hoecake, a Southern term for what other regions may call johnnycake or cornbread, got its name from the way it was sometimes prepared by field hands: They placed the batter on a hoe and held it over an open flame to cook. Today we use a skillet or griddle, but I wouldn't be above using a shovel in a pinch—that's how much I love it. Cornbread is such a big part of Southern cuisine that we've got about fifteen different ways to make it. I like this version because the hoecakes are so thin and delicate, they look like lace.

1 1/2 cups cornmeal
1 teaspoon kosher salt
2 1/4 cups water
peanut oil
cane syrup for serving

In a medium bowl, whisk together the cornmeal and salt. Pour in the water and whisk vigorously for about 3 minutes until the batter is really smooth and very loose.

In a large, well-seasoned, cast-iron skillet, heat 1 1/2 tablespoons oil over medium-low heat. Pour about 1/3 cup batter into the hot oil and quickly and gently press the center of the cake out about 5 inches across. Cook for 5 minutes, until the edges are browned and lacy, then use a thin spatula to flip it, being very gentle with the edges. Cook the other side for 5 minutes, until lightly golden brown with lacy edges, then transfer to the prepared baking sheet to drain. Whisk the batter again before making the next hoecake, and add another 1 1/2 tablespoons of oil to the skillet.

Repeat until you have finished cooking all of the batter, and serve immediately with a drizzle of cane syrup on top.

INGREDIENT NOTE

A traditional Southern sweetener, cane syrup is very sweet, thick, and syrupy, of course.

COOKING TIPS

The batter should look more like that of a crêpe than a pancake batter—the thinner, the better. If you're lucky enough to have one, cook these in a hoecake pan. (A nonstick skillet will do here, too).

ODE TO DAD'S DESSERT

Serves 4

Prep time: 5 minutes
Cook time: zero

I saw my daddy eat this every night for twenty years: He would cut cold butter into cane syrup and spread it on white bread. It was the best thing in the world to him and that's reason enough for me to love it, but the truth is, it actually tastes incredible, too.

¹/₄ cup (¹/₂ stick) cold butter

¹/₄ cup cane syrup

4 slices white bread

Place the butter in a small bowl and drizzle it with the cane syrup. Cut the butter into the syrup and then spread it evenly on the bread.

Bits and Pieces

I have a lot of friends who are artists, and I'm so blown away by their incredible ability to dream up something in their heads and then transfer that idea onto paper. But talking to them, I've realized that drawing is a lot like cooking. To be an artist, you first have to master the basics, gaining an understanding of color, shape, and line. From there, you can move into more non-representational forms. The point is that there is a foundation on which artists build their craft, before they can ever create something beautiful and unique. In the immortal words of Bob Ross, there are such things as "happy accidents," but those are few and far between.

Cooking is a similar art form. Learn the most basic techniques and made-from-scratch sauces and marinades and it will open the door to hundreds of different dishes. The possibilities are endless, but you still have to put one foot before the other in order to pass through that door.

This chapter provides a starting point for home cooks looking to move beyond the jar. Most of the recipes are guidelines for creating your basic sauces and dressings. Others are building blocks for more specific items, like homemade baby food, applesauce, and steel-cut oatmeal. And then there are the compound butters. How do you improve on something like butter? The secret is on page 209—and you'll be surprised by just how easy it is.

This chapter could just as well be the opening for this book—these foundation recipes are so essential. But instead, they're tucked away in the back, like a wonderful secret waiting to be discovered.

NIGHT BEFORE STEEL-CUT OATMEAL

Serves 8

Prep time: 5 minutes
Cook time: 10 minutes (plus standing overnight)

If I can prepare breakfast on Sunday night for Thursday morning and get my kids out the door with most of their clothes on, I consider myself Parent of the year.

If you have kids, oatmeal is probably something you've become reacquainted with—that, and craft paste. These two things, however, should never be confused. That's why I like steel-cut oats. They're better for you, really stand up to cooking, and don't double as a binding agent. But the best part about this recipe is that you can make it ahead of time, keeping it in your fridge throughout the week. To bring it back to life, just reheat it, cutting it with a little cream. We like to set out a buffet of oatmeal fixin's alongside so Jack can add brown sugar plus his choice of nuts and berries.

1 tablespoon butter

2 cups steel-cut oats

7 cups water

1/2 teaspoon kosher salt

1 cup whole milk

optional toppings: berries, nuts, brown sugar, maple syrup, mashed bananas, peanut butter

Melt the butter in a medium saucepan over medium heat. Stir in the oats and toast them, while stirring, until they smell nice and nutty, about 3 minutes. Stir in 6 cups water and your salt and bring the oats to a boil. Once they've reached a boil, turn off the heat, give a final stir, cover with a lid, and call it a night.

The next morning at breakfast time, remove the lid, stir in the milk and remaining cup of water, and slowly bring the oats back up to a simmer, stirring well. Serve the oatmeal hot with whatever toppings you like. Cool down and wrap up any remaining oats in a covered container and place in your refrigerator. Reheat the oats in a saucepan or microwave for breakfast throughout the week.

HOMEMADE CHICKEN STOCK

Makes 1 quart

Prep time: 5 minutes
Cook time: 2 hours

It would be a waste to throw out the leftovers from a roast chicken dinner because I know that I can turn that skin and bones into an entire quart of chicken stock to use for weeks to come—and even longer if I freeze it. This flavorful recipe is just another example of how a little homemade touch can make a big difference in your dishes.

1 leftover chicken carcass

1 large onion, peeled and cut into chunks

1 carrot, scrubbed and cut into chunks

1 stalk celery, cut into chunks

3 sprigs fresh parsley

1 bay leaf

1 teaspoon black peppercorns

3 quarts cold water

Use kitchen shears to cut the chicken carcass into four pieces. Place the chicken in a stockpot with the onion, carrot, celery, parsley, bay leaf, and peppercorns. Cover with the water and bring it up to a simmer, then reduce the heat to low. Cook for 2 hours, skimming the top to remove fat and foam on occasion. (You don't want to boil your stock; instead, just let it bubble gently.)

Allow the stock to cool, then strain and discard the solids. The stock will keep for 1 week in a covered container in your fridge, or up to 6 months in your freezer.

COOKING TIP

Alternatively, you can add all the ingredients to a slow cooker, top with the lid, and cook on low overnight.

WINTER GREEN PESTO

Makes 1½ cups

Prep time: 15 minutes
Cook time: 5 minutes

Everyone is familiar with basil pesto (see page 104), but in the winter months when the price for fresh basil is at a premium, I opt for a seasonal substitution. Kale makes a beautiful, bright pesto that I use in a bunch of different ways. I'll mix it in with some pasta for dinner, spoon it on a baked sweet potato for lunch, spread it on my sandwiches, or swirl it into some sautéed vegetables for a quick side dish. We use pistachios, Jack's favorite, but you can use walnuts, boosting the health factor. Yep, it's a power pesto.

1 bunch kale (8 ounces), stems removed, leaves torn

2 cloves garlic, peeled

½ cup roasted and salted pistachios

½ cup finely grated Parmesan cheese

½ cup extra-virgin olive oil

freshly ground black pepper

Bring a large pot of salted water to a boil. Add the kale by handfuls and boil for about 3 minutes, until soft. With a slotted spoon, transfer to a colander, rinse with cold water, and drain well; set aside to cool. Reserve ¼ cup cooking water.

Once the kale is cool enough to handle, squeeze out all the excess water with a clean kitchen towel. Add the kale to the bowl of a food processor along with the garlic, pistachios, Parmesan, oil, and a big pinch of pepper. Pulse until smooth, then add the reserved water to thin out the pesto.

COOKING TIP

If serving your pesto with pasta, save yourself some time by reusing the blanching water to cook the pasta.

BASIC TOMATO SAUCE

Makes about 6 cups

Prep time: 10 minutes
Cook time: 25 minutes

Make a large pot of this sauce at the start of the week, and all you have to come up with each night is a protein and a pasta to create a wide variety of hearty meals, from primavera, shrimp scampi, and eggplant Parmesan, to beefy mac, or spaghetti and meatballs. Let this fresh and easy sauce be your platform for a headfirst dive into Italian cooking.

2 cans (28 ounces each) whole peeled tomatoes with their juices

3 tablespoons olive oil

1 medium onion, finely chopped

kosher salt and freshly ground black pepper

3 cloves garlic, minced

1/8 teaspoon crushed red pepper flakes

1/2 cup roughly chopped fresh basil leaves

Add the tomatoes to a blender and puree until smooth.

Heat the olive oil in a large saucepan over medium-high heat. Add the onion and sauté until it's softened and just beginning to turn lightly golden brown, about 5 minutes. Season the onion with salt and pepper. Stir in the garlic and red pepper flakes and continue to cook, while stirring, for 1 minute. Pour in the tomatoes, bring 'em to a simmer, and cook on medium heat, stirring on occasion, for 20 minutes. Turn off the heat, season your sauce with salt and pepper, and stir in the basil.

Refrigerate leftovers in an airtight container for up to 1 week, or freeze for up to 3 months.

EASY WHITE SAUCE

Makes about 3 cups

Prep time: 5 minutes
Cook time: 15 minutes

From this basic starting point, you can go in a lot of different directions with this sauce. For example, mix in 1 cup shredded cheddar cheese and you have a creamy cheese sauce that you can use to top steamed veggies and satisfy picky eaters, or add lots of freshly ground black pepper and turn this sauce into a perfect pepper gravy to smother on biscuits.

4 tablespoons butter

1/4 cup all-purpose flour

2 1/2 cups whole milk, warmed

kosher salt and freshly ground black pepper

1/8 teaspoon cayenne pepper

Melt the butter in a medium saucepan over medium heat. Once the butter is melted, sprinkle in the flour, and then stir until the flour is toasted and pasty blond in color, about 3 minutes. Slowly whisk in the milk, season with salt and pepper, and bring the sauce up to a boil. Reduce the heat to a simmer, and cook, stirring on occasion, for 10 to 15 minutes, until thickened and the sauce coats the back of a spoon. Add the cayenne, and adjust any additional salt and pepper to taste.

PIMENTO CHEESE

Makes about 2 cups

Prep time: 5 minutes
Cook time: zero

Most family secrets are best kept under wraps, but not this one. In the name of improving pimento sandwiches around the world, I'm willing to let you in on our secret ingredient: cream cheese. This is one recipe where I encourage you to "double dip": In addition to being one of the most popular sandwiches The Bag Lady ever sold, this spread doubles as a creamy dip.

4 ounces cream cheese, at room temperature

$1/2$ cup mayonnaise

kosher salt and freshly ground black pepper

2 cups grated sharp cheddar cheese

$1/4$ cup chopped pimentos, drained

celery sticks or crackers for serving

In a large bowl, combine the cream cheese and mayonnaise, then season with salt and pepper. Beat with a hand mixer until the dip is completely smooth and light. Add the cheddar and pimentos and beat again until the mixture is well combined.

Serve with celery or crackers or transfer to an airtight container and refrigerate for up to 1 week. If you're making this dip ahead of time, remove it from the refrigerator about a half hour before serving so it can soften up.

INGREDIENT NOTE

For bigger flavor, add 1 tablespoon grated onion and $1/2$ teaspoon garlic powder. If you like a little heat, add a few dashes of hot sauce.

SIMPLE JAM-JAR VINAIGRETTE

Makes 1 cup

Prep time: 5 minutes
Cook time: zero

This basic vinaigrette packs a big flavor punch and isn't weighed down with too much oil or sugar. I like to sprinkle it over fresh leafy greens or sauté vegetables in it. It's also the perfect, light marinade for chicken or white fish.

1 garlic clove, peeled and smashed

1 tablespoon Dijon mustard

$1/4$ cup red wine vinegar (or your choice of vinegar)

$3/4$ cup olive oil

pinch sugar

kosher salt and freshly ground black pepper

Add all of the ingredients to a jam jar and shake it up. Taste for seasoning and adjust as necessary with salt and pepper. Store in an airtight container in the fridge for up to 1 week.

INGREDIENT NOTE

Unleash your inner chemist, playing with different vinegars and seasonings to change up the flavor:

Add 2 teaspoons of chopped herbs for a fresh flavor.
Add 1 tablespoon of mayonnaise for a creamier dressing.
Use lemon juice instead of vinegar.
Add 1 small minced shallot for extra zing.

HOMEMADE BUTTERMILK RANCH DRESSING

Makes about ²/₃ cup

Prep time: 5 minutes (plus optional chilling)
Cook time: zero

President Jimmy Carter told me that his favorite dessert has always been cornbread dipped in buttermilk. I'm a fan of President Carter, but I just can't say the same for buttermilk, y'all. Cornbread is, however, delicious with ranch dressing.

Whenever there was just a bit of mayonnaise left, my mom would make ranch dressing, shaking it up in that very same jar. Now, anytime I'm scraping out the last of the mayonnaise, I think about her, and more times than not, I'll get inspired to throw together this creamy ranch dressing.

¹/₂ cup buttermilk

¹/₄ cup mayonnaise

1 tablespoon white wine vinegar

1 clove garlic, finely chopped

2 tablespoons thinly sliced chives

¹/₂ teaspoon onion powder

1 teaspoon hot sauce

kosher salt and freshly ground black pepper

Add all of the ingredients to a jar and shake it up. If time permits, cover the dressing and refrigerate for 1 hour to allow the flavors to develop. Store in an airtight container in the fridge for up to 1 week.

HOMEMADE ZESTY FRENCH DRESSING

Makes 1 cup

Prep time: 5 minutes (plus optional chilling)
Cook time: zero

My parents always kept a ton of blue cheese dressing at the house, but it wasn't exactly a kid magnet. French dressing, on the other hand, is pretty much universally loved by the three-foot-and-under crowd. Some adults may think this tangy, bright-orange dressing isn't as "fancy" as a balsamic something-or-other, but I bet they've got a bottle stashed away at home. Everyone does. Like my ranch dressing, this recipe is simple to make and holds up really well. You'll also find that it tastes better than the bottled stuff because it's made with ingredients you can pronounce, with one exception: "Worcestershire."

¹/₄ cup canola oil

¹/₄ cup ketchup

3 tablespoons sugar

3 tablespoons white wine vinegar

1 tablespoon mayonnaise

1 tablespoon water

1 teaspoon paprika

1 teaspoon Worcestershire sauce

1 teaspoon Dijon mustard

kosher salt and freshly ground black pepper

Combine all of the ingredients in a jam jar, seal the top, and shake it up. Store in an airtight container in the fridge for up to 1 week.

COOKING TIP

Assemble this dressing an hour before you serve so the flavors have time to come into their own.

HOMEMADE WHIPPED CREAM

Makes about 2 cups

Prep time: 5 minutes
Cook time: zero

I always thought whipped cream should be a dish of its own rather than a topping. It's fluffy, flavorful, and completely addicting. But I suppose because it's so rich, a little bit goes a long way. In fact, it goes so far as to fool your guests—put a dollop on a store-bought pumpkin pie or peach cobbler and it'll taste like a homemade dessert. Or top it on my Peach and Blackberry Cobbler (page 177), Summer Strawberry Oat Crisp (page 167), or Peppermint Hot Cocoa (page 186).

1 cup heavy cream

3 tablespoons confectioners' sugar

1 teaspoon vanilla extract

Pour the cream into the bowl of a stand mixer fitted with the whisk attachment, turn the speed to medium, and whip. Once the cream starts to thicken up, add the sugar and vanilla and beat until medium-firm peaks form.

COOKING TIP

Whip the cream in a bowl that you've chilled in the freezer. I've always used a metal bowl, but you could do it in a glass bowl as long as it's well chilled beforehand. When your whipped cream starts to form peaks, stop. If you whip it too long, you'll have something else altogether: butter. As much as I like butter, I don't want to top my pie with it.

COMPOUND BUTTERS

Making a compound butter is a fancy move that's really simple—a "trick your friends and impress your neighbors" sort of thing. You can really incorporate any flavor into the butter that you want, but I've come up with some foolproof recipes that pair real well with chicken, fish, and steak, especially when they're simply prepared. As soon as the butter melts, it infuses its flavors into the dish, giving it a leg up.

BLACKBERRY COMPOUND BUTTER

Serves 8

Prep time: 5 minutes (plus freezing time)
Cook time: zero

Bobby and I discovered this recipe when we were on the road about ten years ago and we were surprised by how much we liked the berry flavor. It seems like it would be best spread on a muffin or Danish, but it actually pairs really well with a savory steak.

$1/2$ cup (1 stick) unsalted butter, at room temperature

2 heaping tablespoons blackberries

1 teaspoon finely chopped fresh thyme

kosher salt and freshly ground black pepper

Add the softened butter and berries to a medium bowl and mix vigorously, crushing the berries with the back of a rubber spatula. Add the thyme, season with salt and pepper, and mix again to combine. Place tablespoons of the butter down the center of a square piece of parchment paper and roll it up into a log, twisting the ends to secure. Place the butter in the freezer for 30 minutes to firm it up. To use, slice the butter into rounds to top steak, chicken, or fish.

HERB COMPOUND BUTTER

Serves 8

Prep time: 5 minutes (plus freezing time)
Cook time: zero

You can use any herbs you like, but this is my favorite combination to serve on grilled chicken.

½ cup (1 stick) unsalted butter, at room temperature

1 tablespoon each finely chopped fresh parsley, chives, and tarragon

1 clove garlic, minced

kosher salt and freshly ground black pepper

Place the softened butter in a medium bowl and mix in the parsley, chives, tarragon, and garlic. Season the butter with salt and pepper and mix again to combine. Arrange tablespoons of the butter down the center of a square piece of parchment paper and roll it up into a log, twisting the ends to secure. Place the butter in the freezer for 30 minutes to firm it up. To use, slice the butter into rounds to top steak, chicken, or fish.

LEMON COMPOUND BUTTER

Serves 8

Prep time: 5 minutes (plus freezing time)
Cook time: zero

You're going to put lemon and butter on your fish anyway, so you might as well give this tasty trick a try.

½ cup (1 stick) unsalted butter, at room temperature

zest of 1 lemon

1 clove garlic, minced

kosher salt and freshly ground black pepper

Place the softened butter in a medium bowl and mix in the lemon zest and garlic. Season with salt and pepper and mix again to combine. Arrange tablespoons of the butter down the center of a square piece of parchment paper and roll it up into a log, twisting the ends to secure. Place the butter in the freezer for 30 minutes to firm it up.

COOKING TIP

Sometimes I like to roast a filet of fish for 12 minutes, then top it with a pat of this butter during the last 3 minutes of cooking time. It really infuses fish with a bright, citrus flavor.

THE BEST HOMEMADE APPLESAUCE

Makes 1 quart

Prep time: 10 minutes
Cook time: 25 minutes

Y'all, there is a ton of really good organic applesauce out there and it is easy to buy it, but there's something about making our own that we really enjoy. We do it as a family and it's become kind of a tradition in the fall. Some adults dismiss applesauce as "baby food," like it's something reserved for kids who are all gums. But you walk into a house where a batch is being made and I guarantee you'll want some, regardless of your age. If you still need an excuse, you can always pair it with pork chops (see page 200) or a roasted pork loin (see page 80)—but I assure you, real men eat applesauce straight up.

6 large apples, peeled, cored, and cut into chunks (I use a mix of Honeycrisp and Granny Smith)

1 cup apple juice or cider

1 cup water

2 cinnamon sticks

1/4 teaspoon ground cinnamon

2 tablespoons plus 1 teaspoon granulated sugar

2 tablespoons light brown sugar

1/8 teaspoon kosher salt

dash of freshly grated nutmeg

In a large saucepan, combine the apples, juice, water, cinnamon sticks, cinnamon, both sugars, salt, and nutmeg. Bring to a boil over medium heat, then reduce the heat, cover with a lid, and simmer gently for 25 minutes, stirring on occasion, until the apples are extremely soft.

Remove the cinnamon sticks and discard. If you prefer a real smooth applesauce, you can add the apples and liquid to a blender or food processor and blend until it's the consistency you like best.

Store the applesauce, covered, in your refrigerator for up to 5 days. Beyond that, you'll want to freeze it.

INGREDIENT NOTES

You can experiment with the kinds of apples you use, making it milder or more tart. Just make sure you use really crisp apples; nothing mealy will do.

Want more bang for your buck? Add berries. Adding 3/4 cup blueberries to the simmering apples makes this an apple-blueberry sauce.

BROOKE'S BABY FOOD

Brooke saw the first year of our boys' lives as an important opportunity to establish good eating habits. We knew what we didn't want: a battle over food. We didn't want to make four versions of a meal to accommodate picky eaters; likewise, we didn't want to force our children to gag down food they couldn't stomach. We wanted our boys to have a healthy relationship with food—to be willing to try new things and make good choices for themselves.

One of the biggest steps we took toward this goal was making homemade baby food. I've gotta hand it to Brooke, as hard as it was to adjust to having a baby in the house the first time—and then doing it all over again just a couple years later—she made the time to develop homemade baby food recipes for the boys.

She introduced them to a variety of fruits and vegetables through purees that were more flavorful than the watered-down, mass-produced jars. Her purees tasted more like "real" food and I swear it's one of the reasons why they're both such good-natured eaters today. We have our battles for sure, but they're not about food. Consequently, dinner is a big part of our day and one that we enjoy together.

Brooke quickly discovered that between the boys' naps, diaper changes, and playdates, it was difficult to carve out even the littlest bit of time to make homemade meals for the toothless. So instead of trying to puree something for the baby every time we were fixing our dinner, she would make big batches of baby food when she had a minute and freeze the extras into ice-cube trays to thaw when she needed them. That's when I realized that moms in particular are at the mercy of their children's schedule. You can insist on following a schedule all you want, but chances are you won't be the one setting it. Sometimes I'd catch her making food in the middle of the night because one of the boys had woken her and

she couldn't fall back to sleep. That's what parents do: They adapt.

I've also adapted to baby food. When I'm crunched for time in the morning, I take a few of those frozen cubes of sweet potato puree and blend them up, along with a clementine and some ginger, and have myself a fast, satisfying breakfast smoothie. It is surprisingly good.

Today, both of my boys still remember the "food cubes" Brooke would pull out of the fridge and defrost. At the time, we called 'em "dinner"; today we call 'em "Popsicles."

AVOCADO AND BANANA

Makes 1 ice-cube tray

Prep time: 5 minutes (plus freezing time)
Cook time: zero

Think this sounds like a strange combination? Think again. The banana offers a subtle sweetness to the creamy richness of the avocado. This recipe's got it all: a heavy dose of vitamins and the healthy fats little bodies need.

2 large ripe avocados

1 ripe banana, peeled and sliced

Slice the avocados in half, remove the pits, and scoop the flesh into the bowl of a food processor along with the banana. Puree the avocados and banana until they're smooth.

Spoon the mixture into an ice-cube tray and freeze for 4 hours. Pop the cubes out of the tray and place them in freezer bags; label and date. Defrost as needed.

SWEET POTATO AND APPLE

Makes 1 ice-cube tray

Prep time: 5 minutes (plus freezing time)
Cook time: 15 minutes

Don't wait until your child's teeth come in before he enjoys an apple. By pairing pureed apples with mashed sweet potatoes, you're giving your child something that will taste good and stick to his ribs.

1 pound sweet potatoes, peeled and cut into
1¹/₂-inch chunks

2 apples, peeled and cut into 1¹/₂-inch chunks

¹/₃ cup Homemade Chicken Stock (page 205) or water

¹/₄ teaspoon ground cinnamon (optional; for babies about 8 months old and beyond)

Put 2 inches of water in the bottom of a steamer. Add the sweet potatoes and apples to the basket and steam until they're tender, about 12 minutes. Remove the sweet potatoes and apples to a food processor and puree until smooth. Add the stock or water and pulse to loosen up the mixture just a bit. Season with cinnamon, if using.

Cool the puree to room temperature and then spoon it into an ice-cube tray and freeze for 4 hours. Pop the cubes out of the tray and place them in freezer bags; label and date. Defrost as needed.

GET IN MY PANTRY

People always ask me what I keep in my pantry. I suppose it's like wanting to know how fitness trainers stay in shape, or how Tiger Woods wins so many golf tournaments—we want to know the secrets to a person's success.

In my case, there are no secrets in my pantry. I don't have a magic elixir that turns plain dishes into something wonderful (unless it's called salt). I do, however, keep my cupboards stocked with some must-haves. If you're new to cooking, consult this list to get yourself prepped before making the recipes in this book. If you're an old hand in the kitchen, check the expiration dates.

STAPLES

All-purpose flour

This goes without saying. Nonetheless, I'm saying it.

Canned beans

Whether it's kidney beans, white beans, chickpeas, or pinto beans, I keep a stash around for quick soups, stews, chili, or rice and beans.

Canned tomatoes

When you don't have time to dice 'em fresh, canned tomatoes are a good option for soups, stews, chili and the like.

Cornstarch

This fine, powdery starch is a good thickener. It can be used in a pinch if your gravy or stew is not thickening up as desired.

Couscous

These tiny granules of durum wheat are really just quick-cooking pasta. Couscous can be used for salads, stuffing vegetables, or as a simple side dish on its own.

Creamy peanut butter

Peanuts (which are not nuts, but legumes) are a great source of protein, so it's not a big leap to see that this childhood favorite is also nutritious. I keep a jar around for baking or quick after-school snacks—which sometimes is nothing more than a spoonful of the stuff.

Dill relish

The pickled taste is always a great addition to egg, tuna, or my soda cracker salad.

Dried fruits

Cranberries, dried figs, and raisins are great for dressing up salads.

Long-grain white and brown rice

The side dish that's always there for you.

Marinated sun-dried tomatoes packed in oil

Why? Because Brooke tosses them in her meatloaf for a dynamite dinner. Always ready; always prepared.

Nuts

I like to keep a variety of nuts, stored in airtight containers, to add texture and healthy fats to my recipes. My favorites are pecans, sunflower seeds, roasted salted pistachios, roasted salted almonds, and walnuts.

Panko breadcrumbs

I love these extra-crunchy Japanese breadcrumbs.

Pastas

Pasta in the pantry pretty much guarantees that you can make *something* for dinner. I always have a variety of shapes and sizes on hand—rigatoni, penne, linguine, wagon wheels, spaghetti—just to keep things interesting.

Quick-cooking grits

Not to be mistaken for instant, which don't taste nearly as good, quick-cooking grits can provide a dinner or breakfast in more than seven but less than fifteen minutes.

Tomato paste

I always have a can ready to provide a shot here and there for added depth of flavor and an "umami" boost. (That's a borrowed word from the Japanese that means "pleasingly savory taste.")

Yellow cornmeal

A (Southern) necessity.

CONDIMENTS

Dijon mustard

This condiment, which is a combination of ground mustard and seasonings, provides a strong base for many dressings. It also helps to emulsify, or blend, them.

Hot sauce

This refers to anything that's not Sriracha but still gets your attention.

Mayonnaise

Sure, it's most commonly used to moisten a sandwich, but a dollop also goes a long way when making creamy dressings.

Sriracha sauce

More commonly known as "Rooster sauce" because of the bird on the bottle, this spicy chili sauce can be added to just about anything for extra heat.

Soy sauce

Made from fermented soybeans, this salty sauce adds rich flavor to marinades, soups, stews, and sauces.

Worcestershire sauce

A dash of this bold-tasting, fermented condiment adds a depth of flavor interest to soups, stews, and sauces.

Yellow mustard

Use this fat-free flavor-boosting condiment to top sandwiches or rev up sauces.

OILS

Olive oil

I use a basic, less expensive olive oil in most of my recipes for sautéing and roasting.

Extra-virgin olive oil

This high-quality oil is derived from whole, unblemished olives pressed within a day of harvest and has a sharper flavor than regular olive oil. Save this more expensive version for vinaigrettes or for drizzling over a finished dish.

Canola oil

This heart-healthy oil comes from the seeds of the canola plant. Compared with olive oil, it provides a more neutral taste, making it my all-purpose oil for baking, sautéing, and roasting.

Peanut oil

This slightly nutty-tasting oil is ideal for frying. It can be safely heated to incredibly high temperatures, and you can cook multiple foods in the same pan of oil because peanut oil doesn't absorb the flavors of the food.

SPICES

Black peppercorns

Peppercorns, which come from dried, immature berries, are my go-to seasoning. I always make sure I have a refill on hand because running out of pepper is like running out of water.

Kosher salt

I use this coarse-grain, additive-free salt at home and to prepare all of the recipes in this book. It's easy to handle and adheres to food really well.

SWEETENERS

Listen, sugar, there's a bunch of ways to sweeten up a dish. Here are some of my favorite flavor enhancers that are great to have on hand for pancakes, French toast, hoecakes, or to liven up a vinaigrette or roasted vegetables.

Cane syrup

Cane syrup's buttery flavor and golden color isn't as overpowering as molasses and not as sickly sweet as corn syrup. Sadly, there's only a few cane mills still producing this simple syrup in the United States.

Granulated sugar

For all your baking needs. Period.

Honey

Many store-bought versions are made with only a small percentage of real honey, so my family likes to buy local from the farmers' market. You can taste the difference.

Light brown sugar

The addition of molasses turns white sugar into this soft, slightly caramel-flavored staple.

Maple syrup

This sticky amber liquid is made from the sap of certain maple trees. Boiling evaporates the water from the otherwise tasteless sap, giving it that familiar sweet flavor.

Superfine sugar

Because it dissolves quickly, superfine sugar is perfect for sweetening up drinks and cocktails.

VINEGARS

The word "vinegar" is actually derived from the French term *vin aigre*, which means "sour wine." The weak acid, developed through a fermentation process, has literally been around for thousands of years. It has been used as an all-natural cleaning agent and germ killer, but I use it in the kitchen as a base for most dressings and marinades, giving them a clean, flavorful "bite." I recommend keeping a bottle of each of the following vinegars on hand; they have subtle but essential differences. None of them are expensive and they seem to last forever—not thousands of years, but pretty close.

Apple cider vinegar

Made from the fermentation of apples and easily identifiable by its caramel color, apple cider vinegar adds a touch of color and bright flavor to recipes.

Red wine vinegar

This variety is made from red wine that is allowed to ferment. And, you guessed it—it's red, which will also affect the color of your recipes.

Balsamic vinegar

Traditionally made in Italy from unfiltered, unfermented grape juice, this richly colored dark brown vinegar can cost you a pretty penny if you opt for an aged variety, but inexpensive versions abound.

White wine vinegar

Like the flavor of wine vinegar, but don't want to mess with the color of your dressing or marinade? Opt for this clear version made from white wine that also has a somewhat milder taste than the red variety.

SPICE RACK

A good collection of seasonings allows you to spice up any dish, any time. Below is a list of what I keep stocked at home. And as long as you store spices in a cool, dark place, they'll never go bad. They will, however, lose their potency over time. Generally speaking, you can store seasonings for up to six months, so rack 'em up.

Bay leaf

While they look like an herb, bay leaves should be treated like a spice, and as such, perform best when paired with other spices. They're most often found floating lazily in soups.

Cayenne pepper

Not to be confused with chili powder or paprika, cayenne pepper is a pungent, bright red power derived from a variety of chiles. Because it's more finely ground than red pepper flakes, it's ideal to whisk into dressings.

Celery seed

Tiny white celery seeds add a slightly bitter and salty flavor to potato salad and coleslaw.

Chili powder

Unlike chile pepper, which is solely derived from peppers, chili powder also contains garlic and salt.

Cinnamon

Ever complain that something tastes like tree bark? Well, that's cinnamon for you. The ground brown bark of the cinnamon tree gives a warm, woodsy flavor to any dish, sweet or savory.

Cumin

Cumin supplies dishes with a nutty, peppery flavor and is most often found in Mexican and Middle Eastern dishes.

Crushed red pepper flakes

These little flakes pack a hot, smoky flavor. Throw a pinch into a recipe to add heat, just avoid rubbing your eyes afterward.

Curry powder

Synonymous with South Asian cuisine, curry is actually a combination of several spices that are roasted and ground together, including coriander, cumin, mustard seeds, red and black pepper, fenugreek, and turmeric, with possible additions of cinnamon, cloves, and cardamom. I love to use curry powder to brighten up chicken, dressings, and rice.

Dried oregano

The strong flavor of this herb is more pungent dried than fresh. Add a pinch to liven up rubs, sauces, and marinades.

Dry mustard

This powered spice made from the seeds of the mustard plant is a great addition to marinades for beef, pork, and other meats.

Garlic powder

Made up of dried, powdered garlic cloves, this seasoning gives dishes a hint of garlic without the chunky texture.

Nutmeg

At one time, this spice was one of the most prized around. Derived from the seed of the nutmeg tree—a tropical evergreen—the strong, sweet flavor pairs particularly well with squashes and lamb.

Old Bay Seasoning

This spice mix has a cult following among purveyors of seafood, though it's also used on poultry and is great sprinkled over fries. While the spice mix is a closely guarded secret, I'd guess it's a blend of cinnamon, ginger, mustard, bay leaves, celery seed, laurel, and black and red pepper. Save yourself the trouble and just buy this brand.

Paprika

Used in the seventies to pretty-up deviled eggs and potato salad, this spice does have a more practical culinary use. Milder than cayenne or red pepper flakes, paprika adds a palatable kick to dishes without totally knocking you out. The smoked version of this spice is a staple in most Spanish dishes.

CAN'T PUT YOUR FINGER ON IT?

Thanks, y'All

Let's start at the top, shall we? Thank you to Kyle Cathie, the founder of Kyle Books. Kyle reminds me so much of my mother, starting a business and finding her own way to success. I am so thankful and very proud to be a representative of Kyle Books.

Thank you to Anja Schmidt, the lone U.S. employee of Kyle Books. Also a parent in a busy household, she and I really clicked on the direction and tone of our book. Without your guidance, I couldn't have done it.

Thank you to John Kernick and Rizwan Alvi. They are only the top photography team in the business. No big whoop. It was such a pleasure becoming friends with y'all and the result of your work is just beautiful.

A thousand heartfelt thanks to Susie Theodorou and her food styling team, Monica Pierini and Marah Abel. Susie is an artist with food and her work on our book took it to a higher level.

Thanks as well to the rest of the Kyle team: Louise Leffler, Vicki Murrell, Tara O'Sullivan, Nic Jones and David Hearn. Also thanks to Ron Longe for PR guidance.

Thank you to my team at Artist Agency and to my special friend Janis Donnaud, who slid from literary agent to friend about eight years ago. Thank you, Janis, for finding me a wonderful literary home.

Thank you to my two favorite women not named Deen. Brianna Beaudry, who is just the best with recipe development, whether for cookbooks or television shows, and Andrea Goto, who is a masterful writer and knows just the right spot for a comma. We made a hell of a team, ladies.

Thank you to Ray Goto, Andrea's husband, for the illustrations throughout our book. Thank you to Sarah Meighen who, as the perfect assistant, is so important to our family.

Thank you to the City of Savannah, Tybee Island, The University of Georgia, America's Second Harvest, and to our friends at Ottawa Farms and Savannah Bee Company for y'all's continued support.

Thank you to my mom, dad, Aunt Peggy, and my brother, Bobby, for all being important guiding forces in my life.

And to my wife, Brooke, and our two boys, Jack and Matthew, thank you for y'all's support and the best love and kisses in the whole wide world.

JACK'S DEDICATION

To my Mommy
who I love up the sky.